AF612336

ARCHITECTS OF HORROR:

THE HEGEMONY OF DREAD

ARCHITECTS OF HORROR: THE HEGEMONY OF DREAD

The Veiled Archive: E. Lawrence Anderson Literary Research. For permission requests, contact the author at:
elawrenceanderson07@gmail.com

Cover and Interior Design: The Veiled Archive

First Edition: March 2026

Printed in the United States of America

ARCHITECTS OF HORROR: THE HEGEMONY OF DREAD

A Cartography of the Unbroken Chain

PART V: THE CONTEMPORARY VIRTUALITY

The Final Frontiers (2015 – Present)

Foreword: The Audacity of the Blueprint

The standard literary history of horror often feels safe. We trace the lineage from Walpole to Shelley, acknowledge the rise of Poe, and then, with a respectful nod to Lovecraft, declare the genre's evolution complete. This traditional approach treats horror as a mere series of moments—a gallery of monsters and masterpieces arranged in neat, chronological rows for the curious observer. This book rejects that archival comfort. *Architects of Horror* is not a history; it is a structural argument and an intellectual provocation that demands you look far beyond the printed page. Its premise is as audacious as it is absolute: there is no such thing as a new fear. Instead, there exists only the Hegemony, a secret and enduring structural chain where every successful narrative, from the earliest surviving myth to the commercial juggernauts of the late twentieth century, functions as a precise Architectural Handoff.

The true genius of the masters profiled within these pages was never simple invention, but rather a solution. Each great architect—from the Roman magistrate Pliny to the modern systematist Koontz—did not simply create a monster to haunt the shadows; they successfully solved the specific emotional and philosophical limitations left behind by their predecessors. They systemically dismantled the comforting, fragile scaffolding of human order—our laws, our rituals, our faiths, and our sciences—because the intellectual journey of horror demands a final, unblinking confrontation with the meaningless void.

While the following survey is expansive, this list of architects is by no means exhaustive. The work you hold in your hands is, at its core, a structural opinion editorial—an attempt to map and reflect the ancestral roots of the horror we have come to embrace in our modern era. In any cartography of the soul, there will inevitably be omissions. You may find authors who sit higher within your personal Hegemony than they do within mine. Still, that discrepancy only serves to clarify an undeniable truth: we are all influenced, whether as readers or writers, by those who tread the dark paths before us.

This work was a thought experiment born of a forensic study of modern authors' biographies—specifically, those moments when the masters speak with startling candor about who first inspired them to pick up the pen. We all find our spark in the shadow of someone else's fire. If your chosen architects are not found within these pages, I do not see it as an oversight, but as an opportunity for expansion. I encourage you to reach out and share your missing links with me at elawrenceanderson07@gmail.com. Let us explore these overlooked chambers of the edifice together.

This journey is not intended to be easy. It forces us to measure the smallest, most localized ghost story against the vast, terrifying scale of Cosmic Indifference. Yet, by applying this rigorous, almost forensic analysis, *Architects of Horror* reveals the single, undeniable truth of the genre: the chain of dread is unbroken, and the architecture of our most profound fears is eternal. You hold in your hands not merely a record of the past, but the complete structural blueprint for everything that terrifies us in the present moment.

The Unbroken Chain: A Reader's Guide to the Hegemony of Fear

What truly scares you? Is it the image of the vampire's tooth in the darkness, the scream from a haunted house, or the grotesque vision of a body breaking down? We consume horror stories for the rush, yet beneath the surface, every successful jump scare, every lingering psychological dread, and every apocalyptic vision shares the same DNA. This book is about tracing that DNA—the definitive, unbroken chain of intellectual handoffs that created the modern horror story. For millennia, writers have sought to address a fundamental question: How do we make sense of our fear in a world defined by chaos? From the earliest cuneiform tablet to the latest self-published paperback, the source of our terror has been in constant motion. It began as an external, cosmic unknown and has slowly, structurally been internalized. This project, *Architects of Horror*, is the systematic proof of that evolution.

The lineage of dread should not be seen as a museum of outdated terrors. Instead, it serves as a proof of structural necessity, where each major story represents a strategic handoff in an unbroken architectural chain. Every monster, setting, and philosophical crisis that scares us today—from the systemic terror of William Massa to the complex vision of Joshua Bish—is built directly on a structural blueprint crafted by a previous master. To show the full scope of this project, think about the distance between the two figures at the center of our study: Pliny the Younger created the Juridical Specter. This manageable ghost was just an administrative issue for a Roman magistrate. Yet H.P. Lovecraft formalized Cosmicism, arguing that the greatest terror is the moment when the mind faces the incomprehensible, indifferent universe. The 2,000-year journey detailed in these pages answers that exactly.

The "Unbroken Chain" of horror is sustained by three foundational architectures that transform simple scares into a systematic "Hegemony of Fear." The first of these, The Invasive Breach (Pillar A), dictates that horror is a mechanical failure of safety, in which the "Other" acts as a trespasser, violating the sanctuary of law, faith, or the home. This leads directly into The

Symmetrical Debt (Pillar B), a closed loop of consequence in which every terror is a repayment for a past transgression, proving that the lineage of dread is a debt inherited from those who laid the original blueprints. Finally, the journey culminates in The Experimental Psyche (Pillar C), where the focus shifts from external monsters to the trap of the protagonist's own biology and mind. This "Condition" represents the ultimate existential entrapment, in which the "Interface as Skin" fails and the individual is forced to confront the final, devastating realization of a cold, indifferent universe.

Because the intellectual pursuit of this lineage demands structural rigor, this book is divided into two distinct parts. Part I: The Evolution of Horror: A Reader's Guide serves as your essential chronological primer, charting the shift from Proto-Horror through the Gothic, Victorian, and Modern eras. This provides the smooth narrative flow needed to grasp the significant historical events that shaped our fears. Part II: Architects of Horror: Defining the Hegemony goes beyond chronology. This is the structural analysis, where we apply the Lovecraft Metric—our unwavering yardstick—to precisely measure how twenty-one distinct architects systematically dismantled every comforting human system in pursuit of the final cosmic truth. By the end of this journey, you will not only understand why a story is scary, but you will also be able to identify its structural blueprint.

The Unwavering Yardstick: The Lovecraft Metric

To accurately gauge the evolution of this dread, we use a single, consistent standard: the philosophical nihilism of H.P. Lovecraft. Lovecraft, whom we identify as the Hegemonic Apex, described the ultimate terror as the moment the mind faces the infinite, indifferent cosmos. Every architect featured here is judged by their stance on this key question: Is the horror solvable, moral, theological, or cosmic in nature? Our journey traces the gradual breakdown of every comforting human system—law, ritual, faith, science—leading to Lovecraft's final, devastating truth. This analysis provides a framework to demonstrate that all successful modern horror films directly build on this foundational structure. You will know that the monster under the bed is a descendant of the gods of Mesopotamia, and that the domestic tyranny of a modern thriller owes its structure to a corrupt Roman patrician. The question remains: Are you prepared to trace the chain of dread?

The Lexicon of the Hegemony

A Structural Vocabulary for the Unbroken Chain

To navigate the architecture of horror is to understand that fear is not a random occurrence, but a calibrated mechanical result. Throughout this manuscript, different terms are employed to describe the same foundational forces as they adapt to shifting eras—moving from the legalistic language of Rome to the pathological language of the Victorian age, and now to the algorithmic language of today. This lexicon serves as the definitive guide to those distinctions and explains why these structural pillars are essential to the Unbroken Chain.

Pillar A: The Invasive Breach (External/Systemic)

This pillar dictates that horror is a mechanical failure of safety. It functions on the premise that the "Other" acts as a physical or systemic trespasser, violating a protected sanctuary. Depending on the era of the architect, this force is identified as the **Juridical Specter** when dealing with the administrative irregularities of Roman law, or the **Systemic Trap** when the horror is codified by legislative atrocity. As the hegemony moved into the industrial and modern ages, this same force transformed into the **Global Contagion** of epidemiological dread and finally the **Pathological Breach** of the technological era. This pillar is vital because it represents the terror of the External

Predator, proving that no social contract, physical wall, or legal decree can truly guarantee sanctuary once a breach has occurred.

Pillar B: The Symmetrical Debt (Moral Rot)

This pillar identifies a closed loop of consequences in which every act of terror is a response to a past transgression. It asserts that dread is an inherited liability—a "moral rot" that permeates bloodlines, communities, and institutions, demanding an eventual and inevitable balancing of the scales. In a theological context, architects have rendered this as **Bureaucratic Damnation** or **Inevitable Retribution**, where the soul is treated as an account in arrears. In the American context, it manifests as **Inherited Guilt**, the **Ancestral Debt**, or the **Biological Covenant**, where historical crimes are written into the very marrow of the descendants. This pillar is the engine of the Unbroken Chain; it ensures that the "Historical Taint" of the past is never truly buried, creating an inescapable system of entrapment that dictates the fate of the living.

Pillar C: The Experimental Psyche (Internal/Anatomical)

This pillar represents the final inward pivot, where the focus shifts from external monsters to the trap of the protagonist's own biology and mind. It is the ultimate existential entrapment, exploring the moment when the "Interface as Skin" fails. Throughout this work, this internal collapse is described as the **Labyrinth of the Self**, the **Internal Abyss**, or the **Chymical Annex,** where identity is dissolved by substance or madness. In the contemporary era, it expands into **Unreliable Biology** and the **Cognitive Breach**, where the mind is no longer a sanctuary for thought but a labyrinth of self-deception and neurological failure. This pillar is essential because it dismantles the "Fantasy of Bodily Autonomy," proving that the human vessel is merely a temporary host for forces—be they mental, viral, or evolutionary—that the self cannot comprehend or control.

The Lovecraft Metric: A Measure of Nihilism

The Lovecraft Metric is the unwavering yardstick for gauging an architect's philosophical distance from human agency. At one end of the metric sits the **Fantasy of Order**, where horror is Solvable through a magistrate's decree, a scientific cure, or a heroic act of reason. Moving deeper into the chain, we encounter **Theological Certainty**, where horror is Moral; the universe is hostile but just, caring enough about human transgression to render a definitive judgment. The terminal point of the metric is **Cosmicism**, where the universe is revealed as Indifferent. In this state of Meta-Nihilism, human effort and morality are exposed as ephemeral etchings upon an infinitely ancient, uncaring canvas.

Operational Blueprints of Dread

The propagation of the hegemony relies on specific mechanical processes. The **Architectural Handoff** occurs when a new master solves the specific emotional or philosophical limitations of their predecessor, adding a new wing to the house of dread. This often results in the **Banal Apocalypse**, where the monstrous violently irrupts into the mundane rituals of ordinary life, or **Atmospheric Erasure**, where the environment itself ceases to be a backdrop and becomes a sentient, predatory actor. When the fabric of reality itself is compromised, it creates an **Ontological Fissure**, a deviation in the logic of existence that demands the molecular or psychological unmaking of the individual.

PART I: THE FOUNDATIONAL HEGEMONY

The Juridical and Moral Foundations (c. 2100 BC – 1700 CE)

Chapter 1: The Echo of Uruk – Mortality and the Void (c. 2100–1200 BC)

The most merciful thing in the world, as H. P. Lovecraft famously observed, is the profound inability of the human mind to correlate all its contents. This insight, which served as the cornerstone for the modern literary genre of cosmic horror, was not a sudden revelation of the twentieth century; rather, it was the final, terrifying articulation of humanity's oldest written fear, a truth embedded in the very dawn of recorded thought. Long before the Roman specter walked the halls of Athens or the Medieval demon haunted the dreams of the pious, the first terror articulated in literature was the dread of a universe so vast and indifferent that it renders all human effort utterly meaningless, reducing even the mightiest king to dust. The objective start of the literary horror hegemony—the moment existential dread was first inscribed upon the world, a primordial blueprint for all subsequent terror—is found in the harsh, unforgiving deserts of Mesopotamia within the verses of *The Epic of Gilgamesh* (c. 2100–1200 BC).

This ancient mythic poem serves as our conceptual anchor, establishing Mortality, Chaos, and Insignificance as the universal themes that underpin every subsequent literary horror, providing the ancient soil from which the nihilism of Lovecraft's Cosmicism would eventually grow. This primary architectural contribution constitutes a profound statement on Pillar A, delineating an external horror arising from the very structure of the cosmos itself, beyond human agency or comprehension. The epic functions as a brutal chronicle of a hero's crushing realization that there is no law—neither human nor divine—strong enough to counteract the single, terrifying truth that existence is temporary, that all life is fleeting and ultimately inconsequential. We begin with Gilgamesh as the arrogant and tyrannical King of Uruk, a figure two-thirds god and one-third man, whose rule is a testament to the heights of human hubris, a self-imposed divinity destined for cosmic contradiction.

To humble this king, the gods create Enkidu, a primal wild man, yet their eventual friendship only leads to a greater confrontation with the indifferent cosmic bureaucracy, setting the stage for an unavoidable reckoning with universal law. When the gods decree that Enkidu must die, Gilgamesh is forced to witness the first great scene of existential horror in written history: the agonizing, lingering decay of the body, a visceral, undeniable truth of corporeal impermanence. He watches his companion's flesh rot, holding the corpse in a desperate, paralyzed embrace until "worms dropped from his nose"; this image is not a mere detail, it is the absolute, unyielding revelation of physical annihilation, the primordial genesis of body horror. This physical, inescapable end shatters Gilgamesh's arrogance and replaces it with a paralyzing, existential dread, a profound internal collapse triggered by an external truth.

The remainder of the epic is a desperate, failed architectural quest to find Utnapishtim, the immortal survivor of the Great Flood, and reverse the ultimate law of the universe—a futile attempt to build an escape from his own mortality. Gilgamesh returns to Uruk, having failed to achieve immortality, left only with the cold consolation of his city's enduring walls, a physical monument to human endeavor that stands as a stark, insignificant counterpoint to the infinite, uncaring void. The story is a monument to the unsolvable terror of mortality, a truth that no human construct can ever truly overcome. This dread was fundamentally shaped by the political and religious context of Mesopotamia, which operated under a unique concept of a Cosmic Bureaucracy. In this framework, the universe itself was administered by forces inscrutable and indifferent to human suffering. The gods—Anu, Enlil, and Ishtar—were not benevolent protectors in the Abrahamic sense, but fickle, potent entities who treated human beings with outright indifference, their colossal power existing without moral compass or earthly concern.

The horror source was structural: the terror was not a demon or a devil—a figure amenable to human intervention or understanding—but the simple, horrifying knowledge that the most powerful forces in the universe were utterly unconcerned with human life, success, or suffering. The law of the cosmos rested entirely outside of human morality or control, establishing an external threat inherent to existence itself. The gods' decrees, like the flood, were acts of caprice, not justice, underscoring the arbitrary nature of existence—a devastating philosophical premise that negated any possibility of cosmic fairness. This is the theological precursor to Lovecraft's ultimate philosophical position: the gods are alien, vast, and uncaring, embodying a pervasive, absolute Pillar A horror.

While the Mesopotamian tradition grappled with the void of the cosmos, articulating an absolute, external dread, a concurrent, equally vital architectural foundation was being laid within West African Oral Traditions. This global anchor offered a different yet parallel structural solution to the problem of dread, demonstrating the diverse architectural approaches to existential fears. Where the Western tradition, beginning with Gilgamesh, often viewed the supernatural as an intrusion of chaos and an insurmountable external force, these traditions established the Juridical Specter through the mechanisms of Ancestor Veneration and ritual law, framing the supernatural as a functional, often benevolent, component of societal order. The ghost was not merely a frightening apparition designed to haunt the living; it was a functional, structural outlet for finding cosmic and social answers in a world that often lacked human justice, offering a path towards resolution. This introduces the first major veiled contribution to the Hegemony: the concept of the supernatural as an alternative juridical system. In this blueprint, the spirit world serves as a court of last resort, a structural necessity that would eventually cross the Atlantic to define the Black Southern Gothic, offering a contrast to the unsolvable cosmic indifference of Mesopotamia.

The *Epic of Gilgamesh*, though separated from the modern era by four millennia, stands as the purest distillation of the nihilistic philosophy that would eventually define the twentieth century. The terror it articulates is not a localized spiritual haunting, but rather the philosophical horror that H.P. Lovecraft later codified as Cosmicism—a direct, brutal confrontation with truths that shatter the fragile human psyche. Through the lens of the Lovecraft Metric, we see the foundational precursors of environmental dread manifested in the Cursed Space. The Cedar Forest and the abyssal realm of the sea-god Utnapishtim are depicted as inherently hostile, non-human territories governed by monstrous laws that are actively inimical to human presence. The Forest, guarded by Humbaba—whose voice is described as the storm and whose breath is death—is not merely a protected territory but an elemental extension of the environment's inherent malice. This landscape is designed to punish human intrusion, its very fabric an expression of cosmic antipathy that serves as the metaphysical ancestor to the contaminated locales of Lovecraft's Antarctica.

At the core of this Mesopotamian architecture is the ecstasy of decay, a visceral focus on the body's inevitable breakdown that transcends all earthly power. When Gilgamesh is paralyzed by the sight of Enkidu's rotting corpse, he is forced to confront his own physical, finite nature with an unyielding and terrifying clarity. This state of paralysis is not simple grief; it is the absolute shattering of a self-perception built upon the delusion of divinity, replaced by the grim reality of corporeal vulnerability. The specific mention of worms dropping from the nose of the fallen warrior is a primal statement on the biological fate of all flesh, marking the objective beginning of the body horror lineage within the Hegemony. This conceptual chaos functions as the ultimate dismantling of human-derived order, as Gilgamesh discovers that the single, terrifying truth of universal law nullifies kingship and strength.

This realization leads inevitably to the conclusion that a principle of absolute, unsolvable indifference governs the universe. Gilgamesh seeks a rational, ritualistic solution to circumvent the law of mortality by acquiring the plant of youth. Yet, he is defeated by a simple, unthinking natural act when a snake steals the prize. This theft is not an intervention of calculated malice but a demonstration of the universe's arbitrary and uncaring mechanisms—a final, definitive denial of human agency. The *Epic of Gilgamesh* thus defines the maximum threshold of human despair: the terror of the final, unstoppable "No" from a universe that refuses to validate human hope. However, because this dread remained conceptual and mythic, the Hegemony required a new architect to apply this abstract fear to the structures of human society. We therefore leave the wilderness of primordial chaos and turn toward the structured world of the Roman Empire, where the first architect of a recognizable horror narrative, Pliny the Younger, established the Juridical Specter.

Chapter 2: Pliny the Younger: The Juridical Specter: The Curia of Chained Justice

The human intellect inherently recoils from formless chaos, seeking the reassurance of structure and codified understanding instead; the primordial, unquantifiable terror of the cosmos, as established by the preceding epoch, therefore gives way to a dread systematically confined within the rigid strictures of human law. The architectural foundation for modern literary horror thus shifts its focus from the boundless chaos of eternity to the meticulously delineated order of human jurisprudence. The foundational template for the contemporary ghost story manifests not in a work of speculative fiction but in a meticulously documented letter by Gaius Plinius Caecilius Secundus, known to posterity as Pliny the Younger. His correspondence with his esteemed friend Sura, found in *Epistles* 7.27, precisely defines the core contribution of Roman horror: The Terror of Violated Law. This terror, unlike the amorphous, demonic fears of later Gothic narratives, presents itself as tangible evidence of a judicial and moral failure demanding direct, procedural correction. The horror remains localized, resolvable, and inextricably bound to the sanctity of the Roman social order, constituting the first comprehensive addition to the house of horror, a wing of rationalized terror firmly rooted in Pillar A: The Invasive Breach for its reliance on societal structures and Pillar C: The Experimental Psyche for its methodical approach to the inexplicable.

All inexplicable phenomena within the Roman worldview possess an underlying, discoverable cause, reducible to a failure of human adherence to law; Pliny's narrative explicitly presents the supernatural as a mere irregularity within the meticulously ordered human legal system, an aberration that demands not mystical intervention but precise procedural rectification. The text unfolds as a rigorous journalistic inquiry, directly posing the query to Sura regarding the empirical existence of specters, thereby framing the supernatural as a subject for intellectual debate and verifiable truth. Pliny then presents the compelling case of a beautiful, large house in Athens, possessing inherent architectural grandeur, yet rendered commercially valueless, available at a "dirt cheap" price, a direct consequence of a profound haunting. The haunting manifests through an auditory prelude: the relentless, rhythmic clanking of chains, initially distant, then inexorably drawing near, culminating in the visual apparition of a decrepit, emaciated old man, fettered to his legs and chained to his hands. The resolution arrives through Athenodorus, a renowned Stoic philosopher, who, driven by philosophical skepticism, takes up residence in the blighted dwelling. His composed interaction with the specter, a rational gesture commanding the entity to wait, establishes human intellect's dominion over irrational fear.

The specter's subsequent lead to a specific courtyard location, its disappearance, the systematic marking of the spot, the securing of magisterial permission, and the eventual excavation leading to the discovery of a chained skeleton—all these steps affirm the physical, solvable nature of the haunting. The horror dissipates instantly upon the proper burial rites (*iusta funebria*), revealing that dread, within Pliny's framework, functions as an administrative summons, an unsettling but ultimately rectifiable error in the civic ledger, a prime example of Pillar A horror. An individual's worldview, profoundly shaped by their professional identity and societal role, dictates their approach to the terrifying and the unknown; Pliny the Younger's existence was not one of reclusive contemplation but of rigorous public service, embodying the *cursus honorum*, the prescribed trajectory of political advancement. His daily life unfolded within a framework of structure, legal codification, and meticulous documentation, permeating his very perception of reality. His extensive literary output, particularly his ten books of *Epistles*, stands as an intellectual monument, a meticulously curated collection designed to display his administrative acumen and profound understanding of imperial governance, natural phenomena, and ethical dilemmas. The letter to Sura, therefore, does not serve as a fanciful tale intended to induce terror; it represents a professional inclination to scrutinize and classify a phenomenon within a philosophical and legal discourse. Pliny views the supernatural not as a domain for sacerdotal intervention or mystical appeasement, but as a problem awaiting a magistrate's methodical resolution. This administrative lens transforms abstract fear into a quantifiable challenge, reducing the supernatural to a case file awaiting closure, thereby demonstrating a profound intellectual control over potential chaos, a direct manifestation of Pillar C, where the human mind actively seeks to impose order upon the unsettling.

Thematic Anchor: The Stoic Bulwark

The intellectual currents of an era profoundly shape the parameters for understanding and confronting anomalous experiences; Pliny lived during the Silver Age of the Roman Empire, a period characterized by intellectual stability and the pervasive influence of Stoicism. This philosophical doctrine championed rationalism, unwavering self-control, and an abiding faith in a logically ordered universe governed by *logos*. Athenodorus, the central figure in Pliny's account, embodies this Stoic ideal. His calculated composure in the face of the apparition, maintaining his writing, then gesturing for the specter to wait, represents the pinnacle of Stoic virtue: the rational mind's absolute refusal to yield to irrational fear. Pliny meticulously orchestrates the tension between reason and the specter of superstition. Athenodorus decisively resolves the disturbance through the application of an empirical, methodical approach—marking the site, securing official sanction, and initiating excavation—thereby providing irrefutable physical substantiation for the ghost's existence and its ultimate resolution. This narrative functions as a potent affirmation of Roman reason's inherent capacity to master even the most disconcerting supernatural encroachments, systematically dismantling their power through logical inquiry and practical action. The dread dissipates not through magic, but through the rigorous application of human intellect, solidifying this aspect as Pillar C.

Thematic Anchor: Ius Sepulchri: The Right of Burial

The proper disposal of the dead and reverence for ancestral spirits constitute an inviolable cornerstone of societal stability and cosmic harmony; Roman interactions with the deceased centered upon the veneration of the *Manes* (*Di Manes*), the "Good Gods," spirits who, through precise funerary rites and sustained honor, transitioned into benevolent guardians of the family and the state. Proper burial was not merely a social custom; it was an absolute legal and religious imperative, enshrined in the very fabric of Roman life. The *Ius*

Sepulchri, the "Right of Burial," represented a cardinal tenet of Roman law, scrupulously protecting the physical integrity and sanctity of the tomb. A failure to meticulously execute these rites—purification, cremation or inhumation, and the erection of grave markers—resulted in the soul's irrevocable denial of entry into Orcus, the underworld, condemning it instead to an eternal, restless wandering as a *Lemure* or *Larva*, a malevolent, unquiet specter. Such an improperly interred or unburied spirit posed an existential threat not solely to individual tranquility but to the *Pax Deorum*, the "Peace of the Gods," which underwrote the very well-being and prosperity of the entire Roman state. The horror here is a profound societal malady, a metaphysical debt incurred by the living, manifested as a spectral accusation that shatters the foundational peace of the domestic sphere and threatens the cosmic order itself, thus falling squarely under Pillar A for its societal implications and Pillar B: The Symmetrical Debt for the failure of human duty.

Thematic Anchor: Semiotics of the Chain

The physical accoutrements of a spectral manifestation are not arbitrary but serve as potent semiotic indicators, revealing the precise nature of the injustice endured; the specter's most profoundly disturbing characteristic resides in the explicit description of its being bound with fetters and chains. This detail is not incidental; it is the absolute crux that renders Pliny's horror intrinsically Roman and deeply legalistic. In Roman society, shackles were exclusively reserved for enslaved people, convicted criminals, and war captives. A free Roman citizen, by definition, would never be found in such a state of bondage. The chains upon the specter's form function as an immediate, unequivocal signal of a profound and multi-layered injustice: the victim suffered not only murder and the denial of sacred burial rites but was also subjected to the ignominy and dehumanization of being treated as an enslaved person or a criminal during the act of his unlawful death. The chains stand as a visible, excruciating testament to the systemic violation of the Law of the Twelve Tables, the ancient code that meticulously governed burial rights and criminal procedure. The ghost does not require speech; its chained, shackled body articulates a silent, immutable legal brief. The horror inheres in the absolute failure of Roman justice, an unaddressed wound in the very fabric of civic order that precludes the natural world from resetting its balance until the explicit letter of the law has been satisfied. This is a potent manifestation of Pillar B, where societal corruption breeds restless torment.

The domestic space, intended as a sanctuary, becomes a crucible for terror when its foundational sanctity is violated by human transgression; the first element of terror resides within the setting itself: a desirable Athenian *domus*. Pliny's meticulous description notes its “large and spacious” dimensions, yet it is available at a “dirt cheap” price. This economic detail immediately introduces a profound layer of socio-economic dread; the house’s undervalued status signals a hidden, yet profound, flaw—a supernatural defect in its very title that fundamentally overrides its architectural grandeur and prime geographical location. This concept stands as the primordial ancestor of every subsequent “haunted house” narrative. The haunting manifests initially not through visual spectacle but through an insidious aural invasion: the relentless, rhythmic clanking of chains. This sound operates as the auditory manifestation of a past injustice, systematically invading and contaminating the domestic peace. The anticipation, the inexorable approach of the sound, is deployed as a classic technique of suspense, establishing a pervasive dread before any visual confirmation. These sounds are the residual echoes of suffering, permanently scarring the otherwise pleasant environment. The house thus transforms into a monument to unacknowledged crime, its very walls reverberating with a silent scream, revealing the inherent instability of physical spaces when tainted by moral corruption, a clear instance of Pillar A horror where the environment reflects human failing.

True horror does not always emanate from overt malevolence but often from the pitiable, suffering manifestation of unresolved injustice; the specter itself is defined by its abject condition, a masterful subversion of the traditional, imposing figures of classical gods or demons. The ghost is described as "an old man, thin and filthy, with a long beard and disheveled hair," embodying neglect and profound violation rather than formidable power. His unkempt appearance directly contradicts the Roman societal obsession with cleanliness, order, and respectable bearing (the *dignitas* of a citizen). The ghost never utters a single word; its terrifying function is achieved entirely through its appearance and its purposeful actions. It does not threaten physical harm or initiate an attack; it merely points and leads. Its horrifying power stems from its immovable persistence and the undeniable fact that its very existence constitutes an accusation. It demands not a reflexive fear, but a definitive, procedural justice. This pathetic, accusatory presence exposes the raw, unhealed wound of a moral failing, burdening the living with the inescapable weight of past deeds, thereby positioning this spectral entity firmly within Pillar B.

Thematic Anchor: The Lovecraft Metric

The fundamental architecture of universal order dictates the nature and solvability of terror; Pliny's localized, remediable terror stands in stark opposition to the boundless, indifferent, and fundamentally unsolvable Cosmic Horror articulated by H.P. Lovecraft. Pliny's narrative affirms every foundational principle that Lovecraft's Cosmicism systematically denies. In Lovecraft's Mythos, the environment itself is intrinsically hostile; spaces are cursed not by human deed but because the very laws of the universe are fundamentally antithetical to human existence. Pliny's house in Athens, conversely, suffers a curse solely born of human crime; it remains an otherwise beautiful property whose defect is a temporary, removable legal contaminant. The environment maintains its neutrality; the horror is an intruder —an easily purged anomaly — once the human-caused error—the improper burial—is corrected. Lovecraft conceived the physical body as a "galling limitation," a "corporeal cage"; death, for him, represented the gateway to Uncorporeal Liberation. Pliny's corpse, however, functions as a profound symbol of injustice and societal neglect; the ghost is terrifying precisely because it remains inextricably bound to the physical world through its chains and its unburied state. Resolution does not involve achieving formless freedom but restoring the body to its rightful, legal place through proper burial rites. Pliny presents Death as an absolute Legal Obligation.

Lovecraft's ultimate terror manifests as the dissolution of the mind's inherent structure when confronted with the Unknowable; Pliny's story, in profound contrast, stands as an unyielding triumph of Euclidean logic and rational empiricism. The chaos, the haunting, is immediately subjected to the Stoic

Method. Athenodorus employs reason, meticulous observation, and precise measurement to reduce the spectral phenomenon to a simple physical fact: a chained skeleton. The universe remains perfectly logical, its underlying order unimpaired; the disturbance was a temporary, human-caused blip. Pliny affirms The Logic of the Law. Lovecraft's universe is inherently unsolvable, indifferent, and hostile. Pliny's world, in direct opposition, embodies the Fantasy of Order as a tangible reality. His ghost story serves as a profound philosophical affirmation that any breach of order can and must be resolved through human intervention and established legal ritual. The terror is unequivocally solvable. Pliny's narrative is a precise study in Administrative Purging, a testament to humanity's innate capacity to enforce reason and order upon perceived chaos. It fundamentally contrasts with the existential collapse of Lovecraft's cosmos, thereby establishing a critical architectural pillar, Pillar C, in which the efficacy of human reason is paramount.

The fundamental nature of dread evolves in direct correlation with humanity's shifting understanding of cosmic, societal, and moral imperatives; Pliny the Younger's meticulously documented letter stands as the ultimate demonstration of horror's evolution from a discernible legal problem into a spiritual and existential dilemma. By providing the first fully realized narrative of a haunted house and its subsequent exorcism through rational investigation and precise legal rite, Pliny established the fundamental template of the Western ghost story. He cemented the enduring principle that a spirit's restlessness is inextricably tied to an unresolved human injustice. The mystery is systematically solved, and the moral balance of the cosmos is definitively restored. This manageable, juridical horror, framed as a resolvable administrative issue, exerted profound influence over Western narratives for centuries. The Roman template, however, possessed inherent limitations, destined to erode under the pressures of historical change. In the subsequent eras of Late Antiquity and the Medieval period, the centralized legal system of Rome fractured irrevocably, and the prevailing philosophical focus shifted profoundly. The source of failure transformed; it was no longer merely a violation of codified Roman Law, but a grievous transgression against Divine Law. The specter, therefore, must cease its existence as a mere *Manes* demanding specific legal rights, evolving instead into a soul condemned by God—a terrifying spiritual warning demanding immediate repentance. The immediate next step in this horror hegemony arrives with the figure of Apuleius, who introduces the theme of moral transgression and the macabre, internal transformation, meticulously bridging Pliny's external, legalistic fear to the crushing, internalized weight of existential guilt, thereby setting the stage for the Dread of Damnation.

Chapter 3: Apuleius: The Basilica of Moral Abjection

The epochal shift from Pliny's juridical Roman cosmos to the nascent spiritual dread of the Medieval epoch establishes a new locus for horror: the terror inherent within the individual self. Pliny the Younger's documentation of specters affirmed external legal mechanisms as adequate solvents for the problem of the deceased, thereby containing supernatural intrusion within a rational, procedural framework. Lucius Apuleius, philosopher and rhetorician, whose lifespan spanned approximately 125 to 170 CE, subsequently codified a profound apprehension: an intrinsic moral failure inevitably precipitates grotesque, irreversible damnation. His enduring magnum opus, *The Golden Ass*, also known as *Metamorphoses*, represents the sole complete Latin novel to survive from antiquity; it introduces the absolute Horror of Curiosity and the Macabre Transformation as foundational principles, thus establishing the very scaffolding for centuries of ensuing religious guilt and moral dread. Apuleius's work, therefore, marks a distinct architectural contribution to the House of Horror, specifically laying the foundation for Pillar B: The Symmetrical Debt, where the internal transgression becomes the source of an inescapable, punishing reality.

Thematic Anchor: The Macabre Transformation

The novel's central theme asserts the punishing consequence of transgression; this establishes a universe governed by moral retribution, a distinct departure from mere happenstance or external threat. The protagonist, Lucius, a young man of cultivation, embarks upon a journey propelled by an inescapable flaw: an overwhelming, insatiable desire for magical knowledge and practice, universally termed *curiositas*. This intellectual malady drives his initial descent, for it signifies a deliberate affront to established philosophical and societal boundaries. His arrival in Thessaly, a locale renowned for sorcery, places him directly in the crucible of forbidden arts; this environment acts as a magnet for his errant desires. Within Milo's dwelling, Lucius's desperation to witness Pamphile's transformative powers consumes him, overriding all rational restraint and ethical considerations. He compels Fotis, the servant, to acquire a magical unguent. His stated intention involves a graceful avian metamorphosis, a desire for transcendence; however, the ointment induces an accidental transformation into an ass. This physical degradation is an absolute humiliation, a grotesque and profoundly inferior beast of burden, a direct corporeal manifestation of his internal spiritual baseness.

This event is not an ephemeral haunting or a temporary possession; it is a terrifyingly physical punishment, an irrevocable state of being, a complete and systematic dismantling of human dignity. Lucius retains his human consciousness and intellect, trapped inviolably within the monstrous, unyielding corporeal cage of the donkey, a sentient prisoner within his own transformed flesh. This horrific entrapment, where the refined human mind is yoked to a debased, speechless form, generates an inescapable dread of existential degradation and self-annihilation, confirming the dire cost of an insatiable, forbidden inquiry. Lucius's subsequent, desperate search for the sole antidote—a fresh rose—drives the remainder of the picaresque narrative; this quest defines his miserable existence. His life as an ass forces him to observe, from a position of absolute powerlessness, the chaotic circus of sex and violence and the inherent brutality permeating the enslaved person and lower classes. He becomes a passive witness to humanity's depravity, a mirror reflecting his own fallen state. Lucius finally achieves anamorphosis, the restoration to his human form, through the direct, miraculous intervention of the goddess Isis in the final book of the novel. This deliverance marks his ultimate salvation and his subsequent devotion to her as his priest, signifying a complete spiritual reorientation. This salvation is earned only through the complete abandonment of his destructive *curiositas* and the subsequent, disciplined embrace of ascetic faith; such a resolution establishes a clear, albeit arduous, path from damnation to spiritual rebirth.

Thematic Anchor: The Philosopher on Trial

Apuleius's identity as a Platonist philosopher, a skilled rhetorician, and a man publicly accused of sorcery is inextricably bound to the very fabric of his fiction; these elements are not mere biographical footnotes but the intellectual and emotional bedrock of his work. His personal life and the meticulous composition of *The Golden Ass* are inextricably linked by the very fear the novel explores: the inherent danger of occult power and the profound suspicion such practices aroused within the structured order of Roman society. This personal crucible forged the very themes of transgression and consequence within his literary output. The Philosopher on Trial exemplifies the direct correlation between Apuleius's biography and the architecture of his horror. Born into a wealthy family in Roman North Africa, specifically Numidia, Apuleius emerged as a cosmopolitan intellectual. He pursued rigorous studies in rhetoric within Carthage and delved deeply into Platonism in Athens; these academic pursuits reflect an expansive intellectual appetite. His innate *curiositas*, a defining personal characteristic, extended beyond academic philosophy to encompass a profound interest in religion. He became an initiate in several

Greco-Roman mystery cults, seeking esoteric knowledge and spiritual elevation.

The defining event of his life, a trial for magic or sorcery in 158/9 CE, directly informs the terror he later codified. He had married Aemilia Pudentilla, a wealthy widow, and her relatives accused him of employing illegal love magic to enchant her. Apuleius successfully defended himself through a masterful rhetorical performance, meticulously recorded in his *Apologia*. This public trial forced him to articulate a precise distinction between respectable religious ritual, known as theurgy, and illicit magic. This separation forms the unyielding moral spine of *The Golden Ass*. Lucius's traumatic transformation, an unambiguous punishment for seeking forbidden magic, serves as a cautionary tale directly informed by Apuleius's personal brush with Roman law on sorcery, a crime punishable by death. This biographical nexus reveals the profound anxiety over illicit power and divine retribution, forming a central pillar of Apuleius's horror.

Thematic Anchor: The Picaresque of Loss

Written near the apex of the Antonine Dynasty, Apuleius's novel strategically employs Lucius's transformation to satirize the deep-seated anxieties of the Roman Empire, anxieties over status, identity, and control. Lucius, initially presented as an educated, free, and well-to-do traveler, experiences an abrupt and total loss of his status, his linguistic faculty, and his inherent human power. The subsequent picaresque journey through the brutal landscape of Thessaly forces him into the merciless world of enslaved people, thieves, and the lower classes, a stark descent from his privileged existence. The loss of social status and the literal conversion into a domesticated beast of burden function as a direct, horrifying allusion to the pervasive anxieties surrounding institutionalized slavery in the ancient world. Apuleius transforms the societal dread of social fall into a horrifying, extended, and deeply personal literary experience, forcing the reader to inhabit the abject condition of the dehumanized. This narrative architecture solidifies Pillar B by demonstrating how societal anxieties about moral and social transgression manifest as terrifying personal degradation.

Thematic Anchor: Curiositas as the Fatal Flaw

The terror inherent in Apuleius's work shifts profoundly from the systemic failure of the dead, as observed in Pliny's accounts, to the immediate, visceral failure of the living individual. The cultural dread he architects centers resolutely on the instability of human identity and the corrupting, destructive power of forbidden knowledge. This internal focus establishes a new kind of horror, one born of self-inflicted wounds. In Platonic philosophy, curiosity, or *curiositas*, was regarded as a dangerous moral and intellectual vice; it was not a benign impulse but an excessive, illicit desire to know what was hidden, specifically secrets about the divine or the black arts. This philosophical indictment directly fuels the narrative. Apuleius deliberately makes *curiositas* the singular precipitant of Lucius's disaster; it is not merely a catalyst but the very engine of his doom. Philosophical Transgression is thus embodied in Lucius's transformation, a literal manifestation of his soul's degradation and a direct architectural feature of Pillar B: The Symmetrical Debt.

By pursuing illicit magic, Lucius violates the correct philosophical path and transgresses against the natural order of knowledge; his body grotesquely reflects the baseness of his desires, turning him into a base, despised creature. This profound philosophical framework directly lays the groundwork for the emerging Medieval doctrine, where seeking forbidden knowledge constitutes a sin, specifically *superbia* or pride, which inevitably brings divine punishment. This intellectual bridge is direct and undeniable. Societal dread concerning witchcraft was acutely pronounced in Late Antiquity, reflecting deep-seated cultural anxieties. Thessaly, the chosen setting for Lucius's ordeal, was anciently notorious for its sorceresses, such as Pamphile; these figures were not merely fictional constructs but embodied a chaotic, feminine, and irrational threat to the established Roman male-centric order. The Grotesque Body emerges as a central preoccupation, for the narrative features a visceral dread of the skin and the body as a shell, as a prison. Lucius's transformation is a humiliating, irreversible failure of bodily control, an absolute loss of personal sovereignty over one's physical form.

Thematic Anchor: The Hoax Horror

The Hoax Horror, exemplified in the notorious Feast of Laughter incident, showcases a nascent form of macabre deception. Lucius slays three figures he believes are common thugs, only to discover their true nature: inflated wineskins magically animated by the witch Pamphile. This event serves as an early piece of literary macabre and proto-body horror, masterfully confusing reality with the deceptive results of illicit magic. It suggests that reality itself is easily corrupted by supernatural deception, dissolving the boundaries of what is perceived as factual. This architectural element of reality's corruption through moral transgression firmly establishes the pervasive uncertainty and dread that characterize Pillar B. Apuleius's *Metamorphoses* employs the picaresque form not as a whimsical journey, but as a deliberate, relentless mechanism to expose the protagonist to diverse and unceasing forms of dread. This structure ensures no respite from punishment.

The horror of the Corporeal Cage defines the absolute terror; it resides in the invisibility of Lucius's human identity, his intellectual self. Sensory Isolation is a direct consequence of this entrapment: Lucius retains the capacity to think, observe, and rationalize, yet he cannot speak, write, or act upon his thoughts. This sensory isolation constitutes a profound psychological horror, a total, absolute loss of agency and self-determination, reducing him to a sentient object. The Threat of the Other remains central to this horror; Lucius's asinine form signifies his precipitous fall to the status of an enslaved person, a foreigner, or an inferior being, emphasizing extreme social degradation. The terror is amplified by the immutable fact that he witnesses, utterly powerless, the violence, greed, and debauchery of the lower classes, unable to issue a warning or effect an escape. His internal humanity is rendered utterly impotent, a tormenting internal scream.

Thematic Anchor: The Picaresque of Inset Dread

The novel's use of frequent, nested stories functions as a relentless delivery system for localized, concentrated dread. Unceasing Chaos defines Lucius's journey, for the main plot constantly shoves him into new, perilous situations—thieves' dens, brutal masters, lewd priests, and indifferent soldiers. This chaotic, unpredictable sequence maintains an unremitting high level of anxiety, emphasizing that the punishment for *curiositas* is not a singular event but an endless cascade of misfortune and humiliation. The Suspense Mechanism employed by Apuleius further heightens this anxiety; he uses stylistic features, such as the constant deployment of phrases meaning 'all of a sudden' or 'without delay,' which plunge the hero into immediate crisis with no time for preparation or reaction. This rapid, frenetic pacing contrasts sharply with Pliny's slow, methodical buildup of sound, thereby establishing a new, visceral mode of narrative terror.

Salvation from Sin culminates Lucius's ordeal: his transformation ends when he prays desperately to the goddess Isis, who appears in a profound, revelatory vision. The consumption of roses, the promised antidote, is administered by her priest, symbolizing a complete conversion and rebirth into her mystery cult. The cure is religious, ascetic, and total, offering a moral message that the only escape from self-inflicted chaos and moral degradation is faith, repentance, and divine succor. This resolution reasserts a moral order in the universe, albeit one that requires spiritual surrender.

Thematic Anchor: The Lovecraft Metric

Apuleius's horror of grotesque metamorphosis and moral transgression contrasts fundamentally with Lovecraft's dread of indifferent, alien biology and cosmic nihilism. Apuleius establishes a universe that is demonstrably judgmental and chaotic, yet ultimately salvific, offering a path to redemption; Lovecraft, in stark opposition, provides a universe that is utterly nihilistic and eternally damning, devoid of meaning or hope. Environmental Horror, as an architectural element, manifests differently across these authors. In Pliny, the haunted house represents a temporarily contaminated space, an anomaly that can be rectified by legal and rational means. In Lovecraft, the cursed space is metaphysically wrong, governed by non-human, indifferent laws that defy terrestrial understanding. Apuleius's Thessaly is not metaphysically wrong but morally corrupt; Lucius's journey itself becomes the cursed space, a picaresque inferno of human sin and violence. The setting is hostile not because of ancient alien gods or cosmic indifference, but because of pervasive human wickedness—thieves, murderers, abusive owners—which constitutes a resolvable, moral evil, provided the individual seeks redemption.

The Ecstasy of Decay reveals distinct architectural approaches. Lovecraft's Great Old Ones are admired for their formless freedom from the corporeal cage, their abhorrent forms representing a liberation from human physical constraints. Pliny's corpse demands legal recognition and proper burial, affirming human law even in death. Apuleius's Body is the locus of true horror: the punishment of the living body through grotesque metamorphosis. Lucius's change into an ass is the epitome of the Corporeal Cage, trapping the intellect in a despised, repulsive, and uncontrollable form. This dread is fundamentally about the absolute loss of self and status, a psychological rather than a cosmic terror, a direct consequence of moral failure.

Conceptual Chaos presents another point of divergence. Lovecraft's Conceptual Chaos is the terrifying realization that mathematics and science fail, that two plus two does not equal four in the face of cosmic irrationality. Pliny's logic, conversely, affirms the predictable order of Roman law. Apuleius's Logic, however, dictates that the chaos stems directly from a moral and intellectual error—*curiositas*. Lucius's world appears illogical only because he violated the established rules of Platonic and religious order. The logic is ultimately restored by faith, specifically through the intervention of Isis. The final, divine logic is restored, demonstrating that the universe possesses a discernible moral operating system, provided the user follows the correct protocol for initiation and worship. Lovecraft presents the universe as inherently unsolvable, indifferent, and hostile. Apuleius's Order, by contrast, presents a universe that is fundamentally solvable by faith and repentance. Lucius is punished for his *curiositas* but is ultimately rescued by the direct intervention of a benevolent, responsive cosmic power, Isis. The narrative, therefore, offers a clear Fantasy of Religious Order—a distinct path to salvation through repentance and initiation, which contrasts completely with the existential nullification offered by Lovecraft. Apuleius's universe retains its moral scaffolding.

Apuleius's *The Golden Ass* constitutes a critical, indispensable intermediate step in the architectural hegemony of horror, bridging the intellectual chasm between Roman law and emerging Christian theology. By meticulously substituting Pliny's legalistic failure with the profound philosophical transgression of *curiositas*, Apuleius established that the fundamental source of dread originates in the individual's moral choices and internal disposition. The macabre journey of Lucius, trapped within a beast's body, punished explicitly for looking where he should not, created an enduring template for guilt, body horror, and the existential dangers of forbidden knowledge. This harrowing narrative architected a new wing of terror. This theme of self-inflicted moral chaos was perfectly poised for assimilation into the burgeoning Medieval worldview. As the stable Roman legal and philosophical order gradually collapsed, Apuleius's cautionary tale of transgression and subsequent, profound punishment metamorphosed into the universal horror of Sin and Damnation, a theological cornerstone. The subsequent Medieval Text would seize upon this comprehensive framework, transmuting curiosity into the cardinal sin of pride, and Lucius's temporary corporeal cage into the eternal, spiritual prison of hell. The narrative thus became an allegorical blueprint for eternal suffering. The next chapter will explore this seismic shift, in which the moral consequences of a single sin become the central, terrifying spectacle, permanently etched into Western consciousness.

Chapter 4: Pope Gregory the Great: The Basilica of Bureaucratic Damnation

The disintegration of the Roman Empire shattered the philosophical and legal order that had anchored the horror of Pliny the Younger. This collapse created a profound ontological void, severing the established connections between mortal transgression and cosmic consequence. The subsequent Dark Ages demanded a new, overarching framework to govern the terrifying mysteries of the supernatural realm, a system robust enough to supplant the fragmented secular laws. The architect who provided this new framework, shifting the source of dread from the visible, external law to an invisible, internal spiritual accounting, was Pope Gregory I, known as Gregory the Great. His monumental work, the *Dialogues*, irrevocably transformed the classical Juridical Specter into the pervasive Horror of Spiritual Debt. Gregory's central dread is absolute: sin does not constitute a mere moral failing; it is a legally binding, financial liability that the soul must inevitably pay before finding its ultimate rest. This entire construct stands as a foundational monument within Pillar B: The Symmetrical Debt, for its terror originates from the intrinsic corruption of the individual soul and the universal, immutable laws governing its subsequent atonement.

Thematic Anchor: The Horror of Spiritual Debt

The *Dialogues* stands as a definitive collection of miracle stories and supernatural narratives, meticulously compiled by Gregory to serve as a singular source of instruction and comfort during a period of profound chaos and existential uncertainty. The horror, in its purest, most distilled form, is anchored in the stark narrative of Justus, a monk residing within Gregory's own monastery. Justus, a man acknowledged as diligent and generally virtuous, falls gravely ill. While attending to him in his final moments, his brother, Copiosus, discovers that Justus has clandestinely hidden three gold coins. This seemingly trivial offense constitutes a catastrophic, unequivocal violation of the Benedictine vow of poverty, an unbreakable oath representing a direct, unmediated debt owed to God Himself and the sacred monastic rule. The gravity of this transgression is immediate and absolute; it punctures the spiritual integrity of the entire monastic community.

Gregory immediately comprehends the immense spiritual gravity of this transgression, recognizing it as a fundamental rupture in the cosmic order. When Justus dies, the three gold coins ascend from mere material objects to become the undeniable focal point of the haunting, the very embodiment of the unpaid spiritual ledger. The horror is not embodied in the spectral manifestation of Justus himself; it lies in the terrifying, inescapable administrative problem his sin creates for the divine bureaucracy. The prescribed punishment is not physical torment or infernal fire; it is the absolute isolation and communal rejection of the soul, a fate far more terrifying in its implications for the medieval mind. Gregory immediately orders the corpse to be buried alone, outside the sacred confines of consecrated ground, an act of profound spiritual excommunication. The three gold coins are interred with him, serving as tangible, material proof, a binding symbol of his enduring sin and its inescapable financial liability. Furthermore, the assembled monks are compelled to repeat a ritualistic, damning chant: "May your money go with you to destruction," an unequivocal, public declaration of spiritual damnation. After thirty days of continuous masses offered for his suffering soul—the Trigintal—a specific, sustained act of spiritual payment, the spirit of Justus appears to his brother, declaring he is finally "freed from his punishment." The horror ceases only when the spiritual debt is fully and rigorously retired through this prescribed ritual payment, an act of cosmic ledger balancing.

Thematic Anchor: The Administrative Ghost Story

Pope Gregory was a pivotal, indeed foundational, figure who seamlessly bridged the chaotic collapse of Roman administrative authority and the nascent, inevitable rise of the Medieval Papacy. His historical context as a former Roman prefect, a profound theologian, and an intensely practical administrator fundamentally shaped his innovative approach to the terrifying mysteries of the supernatural. The architecture of his horror is a direct consequence of this unique biographical nexus. Gregory was born into a wealthy, patrician Roman family, a lineage steeped in the traditions of civic duty and systemic governance. He initiated his illustrious career in civil service, ultimately ascending to the esteemed position of Prefect of Rome, serving as the city's chief magistrate. This role demanded meticulous record-keeping, strict adherence to legal precedent, and an unwavering commitment to administrative order. He later abandoned his secular life to found a monastery, an institution founded on rigorous rules and communal discipline, and eventually ascended to the Papacy in 590 CE.

This unparalleled background as a meticulous Roman administrator is not simply relevant; it is absolutely crucial to understanding his theological innovations. Gregory authored the *Dialogues* specifically to provide a new source of moral authority and enduring hope during a period of immense turmoil, incessant invasion, and widespread plague, when all earthly institutions crumbled. He strategically deployed the genre of Hagiography—saints' lives and miracle tales—not for mere entertainment, but to systematically replace the failing and fragmented institutions of the Roman state with the unshakable, eternal moral authority of the Church. Under his vision, the Church became the supreme administrative body for the soul. Gregory infused his spiritual narratives with the very legalistic precision and methodical clarity inherent in the Roman civil code. His ghost stories are not chaotic, unstructured folklore; they are meticulously documented case files on spiritual insolvency, each detailing a specific transgression and its corresponding spiritual liability. The fate of Justus, therefore, is not a supernatural anomaly; it is a meticulously detailed administrative process, a divine legal proceeding. The crime, the hidden coins, is identified with absolute clarity. The sentence, the isolation and spiritual curse, is executed with unyielding precision. The debt is systematically paid off over a fixed, calculable period through the Trigintal of Masses, a structured payment plan for the damned.

Thematic Anchor: The Invention of Purgatory

The Justus story is of immense significance because it is one of the earliest and clearest articulations of the theological doctrine that would later evolve into the doctrine of Purgatory. Pliny's ghost presented a physical problem solvable by a physical remedy: exhumation and proper reburial. Apuleius's problem found resolution through personal repentance and direct divine intervention. Gregory, however, architected a new, intermediary system in which the punishment for minor, non-damning sins after death was resolved by the actions of others—specifically, the living monks performing masses. This creation of a middle ground, a purgatorial antechamber between the immediate bliss of eternal Heaven and the absolute horror of eternal Hell, rendered post-mortem dread terrifying but, crucially, manageable through a system of spiritual transactions. Purgatory became the divine debtors' prison, a terrifying but ultimately structured space for the settling of accounts. This bureaucratic rigor provided immense, almost primal, psychological comfort to a population desperately seeking order amidst pervasive chaos; it affirmed a universe governed by knowable, predictable rules, even in the afterlife. The horror lies in the inescapable accountability, not in the arbitrariness of fate.

The most profound and enduring element of Gregory's architectural innovation is the literalization of sin as an unyielding financial debt. The three gold coins discovered with Justus are not merely symbolic of greed; they represent the exact, quantifiable cost of the spiritual transgression, a precise balance due on the soul's ledger. Pliny's horror derived from the violation of the public, legal right of proper burial, an external breach of Roman law. Gregory's horror derives from the absolute violation of a private, spiritual contract—the monastic vow of poverty—a direct breach of divine law. The ghost, or rather the suffering soul, is bound not by physical chains, as was Pliny's specter, but by an unpaid balance sheet, an unfulfilled spiritual obligation. The Trigintal is the specific service rendered and the precise payment required to satisfy this spiritual debt finally. The horror is, therefore, a meticulous, utterly inescapable spiritual foreclosure, a divine repossession of peace until the debt is cleared. The punishment inflicted upon the corpse of Justus, the deliberate act of burying him alone in unconsecrated ground, is deeply symbolic of the communal dread prevalent in the Dark Ages: the terror of absolute isolation and spiritual expulsion. This forced separation from the community of the faithful, both living and dead, represented a primal, existential terror, stripping the individual of identity and belonging.

Thematic Anchor: The Specter as Evidence

Gregory unequivocally completes the conversion of the classical ghost into the uniquely Medieval, fully accountable soul. The apparition that ultimately appears to Copiosus, Justus's brother, is not malevolent, vengeful, or chaotic in its manifestations; it functions as a spectral accountant, appearing solely to confirm that the spiritual ledger has been meticulously settled. This profound transformation of the animating spirit—from a chaotic, vengeful Larva of Roman folklore to an auditable, suffering soul yet ultimately redeemable—is Gregory's greatest and most enduring architectural contribution. The specter becomes a report, a confirmation, devoid of agency beyond its role in validating a transaction. Gregory's terror mechanics are exquisitely designed to induce pervasive spiritual conformity through a rigorously bureaucratic narrative, one that deliberately strips away the dramatic spectacle and chaotic agency often found in earlier horror traditions. The horror resides in the system's inexorable, impersonal logic. The mechanics of humiliation used against Justus rely entirely on public shame and legal expulsion from the sacred community. Gregory orders the monks to parade the three gold coins before the assembled community, ensuring the nature of the transgression is unequivocally clear to all, rendering Justus a perpetual example of spiritual bankruptcy.

Unlike Pliny's chained specter, which rattled its fetters and gestured with ominous intent, the monk Justus remains utterly silent during the entire duration of his punishment. His suffering is not articulated; it is implied by his absolute isolation and the ritualistic cursing directed at his memory. When he finally appears to Copiosus, it is only to confirm the successful conclusion of the Trigintal and to deliver an accounting update. The silence of the suffering soul introduces a new, chilling source of dread: the agony must be inferred, imagined, and internalized by the living, rather than explicitly witnessed, making the horror far more insidious and personal. This silence accentuates the interaction's bureaucratic, data-entry nature. The resolution mechanism Gregory constructs is a sophisticated, administrative process that is precise and predictable. A one-time physical act of reburial cured Pliny's problem. A sustained, continuous service cures Gregory's problem: thirty consecutive Masses. The solution demands time, consistency, and communal effort—a bureaucratic, methodical solution for an intensely spiritual problem.

Thematic Anchor: The Lovecraft Metric

Pope Gregory the Great's ordered, entirely accountable universe stands in absolute, fundamental opposition to Lovecraft's nihilistic cosmos, providing a necessary and complete counterpoint to the terrifying cosmic void. Gregory's architecture affirms meaning; Lovecraft's dissolves it. Environmental horror in Lovecraft's works, such as the sunken city of R'lyeh, is cursed by non-human geometry and an intrinsic, indifferent malevolence. Gregory's space, such as the unconsecrated grave of Justus, is cursed solely by the spiritual contamination of sin, a moral defilement. The ground becomes hostile and terrifying only because of the unpurged spiritual debt it bears. Once the debt is paid, the space immediately becomes neutral, devoid of any residual malevolence, definitively proving that the horror is entirely moral, entirely transactional, and entirely dependent on the state of the soul's account. The landscape itself is merely a canvas for human spiritual accounting.

Regarding the body, Lovecraft often seeks Uncorporeal Liberation, viewing the flesh as a limitation. Gregory's body, specifically the corpse of Justus, is treated as a piece of contaminated property, a vessel holding a spiritual debt. It is cursed and deliberately buried with the physical manifestation of the sin—the coins—to actively prevent the spiritual debt from corrupting the living community. The flesh is merely a ledger entry, subject to a spiritual lien. While Lovecraft's conceptual chaos shatters the human mind by proving that the universe's fundamental logic is alien and incomprehensible, Gregory's logic is defined by perfect, utterly predictable accounting. The spiritual world operates under the same meticulous rules as the Roman treasury. Sin equals Debt; Ritual equals Payment. This system of precise spiritual reckoning is the absolute antithesis of Lovecraft's nihilistic void. Lovecraft's cosmos is inherently unsolvable, whereas Gregory's order offers a solvable horror through communal action and adherence to established spiritual protocols. The creation of Purgatory is the ultimate Fantasy of Order, reinforcing the Church's supreme authority as the arbiter of this divine system.

Pope Gregory the Great stands as the vital, structural architect who meticulously secured the continuity of the horror hegemony across the tumultuous expanse of the Dark Ages. He successfully transitioned the horror narrative from the external, public legalism of Rome to the internal, exacting Early Medieval system of spiritual debt, thereby establishing a terrifying new dimension of post-mortem accountability. His monumental creation of an accountable afterlife and the systematic management of spectral suffering established the terrifying certainty that every sin, no matter its perceived insignificance, created a permanent, addressable liability upon the soul. This architectural innovation firmly places Gregory's work within Pillar B: The Symmetrical Debt, as the dread arises intrinsically from the individual's spiritual decay, subject to an unwavering divine bureaucracy. Gregory's meticulously designed system, however, retained a crucial element of solvability. The next inevitable step in the architectural evolution of horror demanded the systematic shattering of that hope, introducing the concept of absolute, unforgivable damnation. This necessitates a fundamental shift from the curable debt Gregory defined to the soul's final, irrevocable foreclosure. The next architect in this grand design, William of Malmesbury, provides the gruesome, public spectacle required to cement this new, harsher reality.

Chapter 5: William of Malmesbury: The Cloister of Inevitable Retribution

The fabric of the cosmos, as understood by the nascent medieval intellect, presented a profound dilemma following the erosion of classical certitudes: could the earnest devotion of humanity truly counteract the corrosive omnipresence of sin? This fundamental theological query received its chilling, irrefutable pronouncement through the meticulously chronicled narratives of William of Malmesbury. His infamous account of "The Witch of Berkeley," penned around 1125 CE, serves not merely as an anecdotal record but as a foundational architectural blueprint for medieval dread, meticulously constructed to demonstrate the absolute impotence of all human and sacred ritual in the face of mortal transgression. This narrative performs the critical Structural Handoff, transitioning the conceptualization of spiritual culpability from Pope Gregory's curable Spiritual Debt—a manageable, albeit grave, ledger entry—to an absolute, unforgivable Damnation, a foreclosure of the soul's very essence that Dante Alighieri would later systematize into a cosmic jurisprudence. The very ground of spiritual recourse shifts; a chasm opens where once a path to penance lay.

Thematic Anchor: The Horror of Ritual Failure

William of Malmesbury, a Benedictine monk of considerable erudition and a historian of unparalleled repute, consciously embeds the story of the Witch of Berkeley within the grand historical sweep of his *Gesta Regum Anglorum* as a pivotal didactic digression. The inherent horror of this narrative rests on the inescapable, ironclad certainty of eternal judgment, a judgment rendered immutable by absolute moral rot. The central figure, a woman of significant means residing in Gloucestershire, exemplifies this profound moral decay; she exists in a state of unrepentant addiction to sorcery, augury, and a spectrum of corporeal vices, described with chilling precision as "excessively gluttonous, perfectly lascivious." Upon receipt of a dark, unmistakable omen, she recognizes her imminent demise and, crucially, the preordained certainty of her damnation. Her subsequent confession is not an act of contrition seeking absolution, but a terrifying recognition of an irreversible spiritual contract. Knowing her soul is irredeemably lost, she turns her desperate pleas toward her children, a monk and a nun, imploring them to enact a series of elaborate protections for her physical remains, hoping to shield her body from the demons assembling to claim their due. This desperate plea against an already sealed fate illustrates the dawning terror of a system where internal corruption, Pillar B: The Symmetrical Debt, renders even the most sacred external safeguards utterly void.

Her instructions delineate a meticulous, almost frantic, concatenation of ritualistic defense: her corpse must be sewn into the hide of a stag, placed within a heavy stone coffin, this coffin then bound by three massive iron chains, and finally, a continuous, unbroken vigil must be maintained with ceaseless psalms and fifty masses offered over three successive nights within the hallowed confines of the church. These are not mere superstitions; these are the very apogee of sacred human defense mechanisms. Yet, the ritual fails with a devastating, absolute finality. On the first two nights, the infernal agents, manifesting with escalating, inexorable power, effortlessly shatter two of the massive chains. On the third night, the climactic assault arrives; a demon, "more terrible in appearance than the rest," ruptures the final chain with devastating ease, "as though it had been made of flax." This supreme entity shatters the very doors of the church, violating the sanctity of the sacred space, and, with an act of primordial terror, forcibly drags the woman's corpse from her coffin. She is then mounted upon a horrifying black horse, adorned with cruel iron hooks, and vanishes into the night, her terrified pleas echoing for miles across the darkened landscape. The horror is thus made manifest and complete: absolute sin renders all human piety and sacred defense entirely ineffectual.

Thematic Anchor: The Sinner's Contrapasso

William's tale meticulously engineers its terror mechanics to be explicitly cinematic and profoundly visceral. It definitively supplants the subtle, creeping psychological dread of earlier periods with a terrifying, absolute final judgment. This shift represents a deliberate architectural choice, moving from suggestion to undeniable spectacle, placing the consequences of Pillar B directly before the audience's eyes. The narrative of the Witch of Berkeley definitively marks The End of Solvable Spiritual Debt. Gregory's theological framework allowed for spiritual sin to be conceptualized as a manageable debt addressable through a Trigintal. William's tale shatters this fragile hope. The Witch's confession of her "enslavement to the artifice of the devil" functions as the literary acknowledgement of an irrevocable contract; the moral ledger is no longer an account merely payable to the purgatorial realms, but a foreclosed contract, irrevocably owned by Hell itself. The transgression articulated here is a deliberate, unpardonable covenant with the demonic, a pact so absolute that it provides the necessary theological severity and structural precedent for Dante's later, meticulously precise, and eternal tortures.

This story meticulously delineates the nascent form of contrapasso. William explicitly emphasizes her egregious sins—gluttony, lasciviousness, augury—thereby establishing with irrefutable clarity that her punishment is not arbitrary, but entirely justified, a direct and proportional consequence of her moral choices. The profound moral degradation of her soul so thoroughly contaminates her physical body that it becomes an intolerable, repulsive entity, utterly unfit for hallowed ground. This concept, that spiritual sin manifests as a tangible physical repulsion and necessitates a physical cleansing from sacred space, precisely establishes the gruesome, retributive logic of contrapasso. The body itself becomes an extension of the soul's damnation, a physical placeholder for eternal torment. The core of this horror is The Spectacle of Ritualistic Defeat, the public and undeniable demonstration that human piety, however fervent, is ultimately futile against the overwhelming force of absolute evil when that evil has been willingly embraced. The casual, almost effortless destruction of these defenses by the demonic agents is the foundational spectacle of terror.

Thematic Anchor: The Forced Expulsion from Hallowed Ground

The final, horrifying act, The Forced Expulsion from Hallowed Ground, constitutes the ultimate horror for the medieval mind. The body, violently dragged from the sanctity of the church, is a public and undeniable manifestation of eternal rejection. This act confirms the soul's absolute forfeiture by denying the body its fundamental right to rest within consecrated earth, a visceral reversal of Pliny's successful internment that promised peace. This forceful abduction establishes a new, terrifying precedent: the spiritual landscape itself becomes a site of active, violent judgment, where the damned find no terrestrial refuge. The narrative employs The Mechanics of Grotesque Violence with escalating intensity and overwhelming sensory overload. The siege upon the church does not commence with gentle, spectral manifestations; it erupts with the terrifying "clamor of the approaching enemy" that physically shakes the entire monastery. This aggressive aural intensity stands in stark contrast to the gentle clanking of Pliny's specter's chains. Here, the corpse is not merely disturbed; it is violently resurrected, its enforced reanimation serving as a prelude to an eternity of physical pain.

Crucially, the priests and observers within the besieged church are rendered entirely motionless, paralyzed by overwhelming terror. Unlike the calm, philosophical Athenodorus, who actively intervened in Pliny's narrative, these holy men are reduced to passive, horrified spectators. Their profound inability to act or offer solace underscores the absolute authority of divine judgment. It highlights the profound, terrifying helplessness of human piety when confronted with absolute evil and an irrevocably damned soul. This paralysis underscores the unyielding nature of the judgment, affirming that the spiritual battle is already lost, the fate sealed by moral rot, leaving no room for human intercession.

Thematic Anchor: The Lovecraft Metric

William of Malmesbury's meticulously ordered world is entirely dominated by a theological certainty, a universe governed by absolute moral law and divine decree. This stands in sharp, categorical opposition to Lovecraft's universe, characterized by cosmic chance and overwhelming indifference. The chronicler's horror is systematic because it is fundamentally deserved, a precise calculation of moral consequence. Lovecraft's horror, conversely, is arbitrary, unsettling precisely because it is uncaring. In William's conception of Environmental Horror, the space itself becomes theologically hostile. The church, understood as the most sacred Christian sanctuary, is revealed to be completely vulnerable to the overwhelming power of Hell's agents. The terror is rooted in the profound fear that the established Christian order cannot guarantee safety when faced with absolute sin. This is a crucial element of Pillar B, where moral rot within an individual compromises even the most hallowed external spaces. Lovecraft's environments are metaphysically wrong because of alien laws; William's church suffers a permanent spiritual breach, its sanctity irrevocably compromised by the intrinsic evil it seeks to contain.

In William's narrative, the body is the ultimate physical representation of the soul's absolute forfeiture. The horror manifests in the violent denial of natural decay and restorative rest. The corpse is violently snatched and re-animated for the express purpose of eternal, targeted torment. The body becomes a living tomb, a vessel of perpetual suffering, directly reflecting the moral rot that permeated its earthly existence. Concerning Conceptual Chaos, Lovecraft's cosmic horror shatters the human mind by revealing that the fundamental logic of the universe is alien. William's logic is one of absolute, unyielding moral order. The witch possesses a complete, terrifying understanding of her fate precisely because the spiritual mathematics are sound: absolute Sin equates directly and irrevocably to Damnation. The universe is not indifferent; it is terrifyingly just, ensuring Pillar B's inescapable execution. Finally, while Pope Gregory's spiritual debt was solvable, William's order presents a horror that is fundamentally unsolvable by human will or ritual once a certain threshold of sin is crossed. The tale functions as a horrifying Fantasy of Moral Order—the universe does not simply exist; it cares with an active, terrifying intensity about human choice.

William of Malmesbury's chilling narrative provides the critical, definitive handoff from the realm of the solvable spiritual system to the absolute, unforgivable foreclosure of the soul. His tale stands as the gruesome historical proof that when sin reaches a certain magnitude, when moral rot infects the very core of being, the spiritual system collapses, and the only remaining certainty is the inevitability of systematic punishment. By chronicling the final, undeniable failure of Christian ritual to save a damned soul, he irrevocably paved the way for the ultimate terror of the Medieval period: the fully organized, inescapable, and architecturally precise Hell. This gruesome, physical spectacle—the tearing iron hooks, the shattering chains, the public shrieking—demanded a systematic literary accounting, a detailed mapping of infernal geography. The next architect to enter this burgeoning house of horrors, Canon Marcus, takes William of Malmesbury's crude account and refines it into a sophisticated, detailed tour of Hell. This pioneering vision literature will establish the meticulous architecture of the afterlife, a structural framework of punishment that Dante Alighieri will later refine into his philosophical system of contrapasso.

Chapter 6: Canon Marcus: The Cartography of the Visceral Ledger

The gruesome spectacle of the Witch of Berkeley, as chronicled by William of Malmesbury, established a terrifying new reality: the absolute foreclosure of the soul. However, while William provided the visceral proof of ritual failure, the infernal landscape remained a fragmented, encroaching shadow, a series of disconnected horrors lacking a unified spatial logic. It was the Irish monk Canon Marcus, writing in the mid-12th century, who transformed this shadow into a rigorous, detailed blueprint. Through his primary work, *The Vision of Tundale* (*Visio Tnugdali*), Marcus performs the critical Forensic Handoff, evolving medieval dread from a singular narrative event into a systematic, catalogued geography of pain. He is the architect who takes the shattered chains of the Berkeley church and uses them to forge the first truly organized house of horrors.

Thematic Anchor: The Inventory of Agony

Marcus's narrative follows Tundale, a wicked knight of noble birth but ignoble spirit, who falls into a death-like trance and is led by a guardian angel through the topography of the afterlife. Unlike the brief, panicked glimpses of judgment found in earlier accounts, Marcus provides a relentless, itemized Inventory of Agony. He moves the reader through a series of specialized environments: mountains of fire, valleys of ice, and pits of sulfur. This is the first significant emergence of The Functional Architecture of Hell—the realization that the afterlife is not merely a void of suffering. Still, a series of designed chambers, each meticulously built to process a specific grade of moral rot.

The terror here is no longer a temporary "breach" into the mortal world; instead, the sinner is forcefully integrated into the permanent mechanics of the infernal. Marcus describes a massive, glowing iron grid where the souls of the damned are melted together into a single, screaming mass of molten humanity, only to be strained through a metaphorical sieve and reformed for further torment. This represents a pivotal shift in the Mechanics of Grotesque Violence: the body is no longer a vessel to be protected by sacred ritual, but the raw material for an eternal, industrial process of retribution.

Thematic Anchor: The Angelic Custodian: The Clerk of the Pit

While the witnesses in William of Malmesbury's church were reduced to a state of terrified, motionless paralysis, Marcus introduces a more unsettling form of observation through the figure of the Angelic Custodian. This entity does not offer the "Spiritual Recourse" one might expect from a divine messenger; instead, he functions as a Clerk of the Infernal Court. As Tundale is dragged through the topography of the pit, the Angel provides a chillingly detached commentary on the Symmetrical Debt being extracted from each soul.

The horror here is not found in the Angel's wrath, but in his Administrative Indifference. When Tundale pleads for mercy, the Angel does not offer absolution; he offers a "forensic" explanation of why the torture is mathematically necessary based on the sinner's earthly "Moral Rot". This marks a definitive shift in the Hegemony of Horror: the divine is no longer a source of comfort but rather the ultimate, unyielding logic that governs the prison. The Angel represents the "Unwavering Yardstick" in motion. This being ensures that the Cartography of the Unbroken Chain is followed to the letter, stripping away any hope of divine intervention or clerical error.

Thematic Anchor: The Symmetrical Punishment and the Beast Acheron

If William of Malmesbury established that sin was a debt that could not be paid, Canon Marcus begins to define the Specific Interest on that debt. He introduces the nascent logic of *contrapasso* that Dante would later elevate to a philosophical law. A primary example is the encounter with the Beast Acheron—a creature of such gargantuan proportions that its eyes glow like pillars of fire and its mouth can hold nine thousand men.

Those who succumbed to the "Pillar B" rot of gluttony and avarice are swallowed by this entity, where they are digested by inner fires and gnawed upon by serpents. This is the birth of The Symmetrical Ledger. Marcus demonstrates that the "Hegemony of Horror" is essentially administrative in nature. The punishment is no longer an arbitrary lashing by demons; it is a direct, physiological consequence of the sin itself. The "Moral Rot" is rendered as a biological reality: the sinner's body is literally consumed by the vices it once housed, making the environment of the pit an extension of the sinner's own internal corruption.

Thematic Anchor: The Valley of Thermal Extremes: The Kinetic Agony

Marcus expands the Inventory of Agony by describing the Valley of Thermal Extremes. In this place, souls are tossed between a mountain of searing, volcanic fire and a mountain of soul-chilling, absolute ice. This is not merely a display of physical pain; it is a Metaphysical Displacement. In the Lovecraft Metric, this environment is "wrong" because it denies the body any state of equilibrium, stripping away the possibility of adapting to the suffering.

The sinners here, described as those who were "neither hot nor cold" in their devotion, suffer a Kinetic Retribution. They are perpetually on the move, never allowed the Restorative Rest that Pliny's ghost sought in earlier centuries. This architectural choice by Marcus creates a sense of Perpetual Flux, where the body becomes a site of conflicting elemental forces. The "Environmental Horror" is total; the very air the damned breathe is an instrument of the state's judgment, proving that Pillar B's consequences extend to the literal atoms of the afterlife, leaving no terrestrial or celestial refuge.

Thematic Anchor: The Test of the Iron Bridge

Marcus further refines the architecture of dread through the Test of the Iron Bridge. Tundale is forced to lead a wild cow across a bridge two miles long and only a hand's breadth wide, studded with razor-sharp nails. Beneath him lies a lake of sulfurous fire filled with hungry beasts. This architectural feature serves as a Metaphorical Sieve, a mechanical sorting of souls based on the weight of their transgressions.

This is the transition from William's "Spectacle of Defeat" to Marcus's "Catalog of Consequence". It provides the necessary structural foundation for a universe where judgment is not just certain, but meticulously categorized. The bridge is a physical manifestation of the narrow path of righteousness, where the Symmetrical Debt becomes a matter of literal balance and physical endurance. The failure to cross is not a stroke of bad luck; it is a mathematical certainty for those whose souls are heavy with unrepentant sin, a public demonstration that the spiritual battle was already lost before the first step was taken.

Thematic Anchor: The Metallurgy of the Damned: The Forge of Identity

The ultimate expression of Marcus's industrial horror is found in the Smithy of Phistiamus. Here, demons act as blacksmiths, using massive bellows to stoke the "Fires of Inquiry" and heavy tongs to place souls upon the Anvil of Erasure. Marcus describes twenty or thirty souls being hammered together into a single, glowing mass of agony, only to be shattered apart and reforged for a new cycle of torment.

This process represents the Foreclosure of the Individual. In the "Veiled Archive," this is the first moment where horror moves from the punishment of the body to the Destruction of the Self. The anvil is a site of literal "Moral Metallurgy," where the "Moral Rot" is hammered out of the soul through a process of shattering and reconstruction. This is the precursor to the psychological horrors of the modern age—the realization that the "Hegemony" can not only punish you but can fundamentally remake you in a forge of its own design, erasing the "Unbroken Chain" of your own history to replace it with a monument of perpetual suffering.

Thematic Anchor: The Lovecraft Metric

In the Lovecraft Metric, Marcus's vision occupies a space of Theological Hostility. While Lovecraft's environments are alien and indifferent, Marcus's Hell is obsessively attentive. The sulfurous pits and the iron bridges are not natural features of a chaotic void; they are a Fantasy of Moral Order made manifest. The universe is revealed to be an inescapable, judgmental machine.

Concerning **Conceptual Chaos**, Marcus replaces the psychological dread of the unknown with the crushing weight of the known. The horror is found in the Absolute Fixity of the system. Once Tundale crosses the bridge, the logic of the universe is revealed to be unyielding. There is no "cosmic chance" here; there is only the "Unwavering Yardstick" of divine decree. Marcus's contribution to the Unbroken Chain is the assurance that the architecture of dread is stable, permanent, and terrifyingly efficient, ensuring that Pillar B's inescapable execution is the only remaining logic.

The Evolutionary Handoff: The Blueprint for the Poet

Canon Marcus's sprawling, visceral tour provided the raw, descriptive data that the Medieval mind required to visualize its deepest fears. He took the "foreclosed soul" of William of Malmesbury and gave it a permanent, itemized residence. However, while Marcus provided the *map*, he lacked the ultimate *jurisprudence*. His Hell was a collection of horrors, but it was not yet a perfect, closed system of law.

The handoff now moves from the monk's visceral catalog to the scholar's philosophical system. The raw materials of the molten grid, the thermal valleys, and the river of blood are ready to be refined. The next architect, Dante Alighieri, will take Canon Marcus's crude cartography and turn it into a geometrically perfect prison of absolute justice, completing the theological architecture of the Unbroken Chain and setting the stage for the secularization of dread.

Chapter 7: Dante Alighieri: The Architecture of Eternal Punishment: The Infernal Blueprint of Absolute Justice

The Medieval Age of Dread found its foundational articulation in a series of literary works, each of which meticulously defined the nature and remediation of existential suffering. Pliny established the problem's curability through Law, suggesting a societal framework for human transgression; Gregory advanced the notion of spiritual debt as a redeemable condition, positing a path to divine reconciliation; Tundale then presented a visceral, catalogued compendium of tortures, illustrating the horrifying consequences of sin with stark imagery. The final, most ambitious architect to emerge from this era was Dante Alighieri, whose epic, *Inferno*, transcended mere spectacle, transforming the realm of Hell into a perfect, philosophical system. Dante's prodigious work provided ultimate theological closure, delivering the assurance that cosmic judgment was not arbitrary or capricious, but impeccably, terrifyingly just. This terrifying certainty concludes the Theological Age of Dread, compelling the hegemony of horror to seek its new, potent sources of fear within the burgeoning human experience of the Gothic era, marking a decisive shift from divine decree to terrestrial terror. Dante's edifice stands as a monumental testament to Pillar B: The Symmetrical Debt, the inescapable consequence of Moral Rot, demonstrating how internal corruption finds its perfect, externalized architectural reflection.

Thematic Anchor: The Architecture of Eternal Punishment

Dante's *Inferno*, the inaugural canticle of his *Divine Comedy*, unfolds as the harrowing account of its protagonist, Dante, who undertakes a perilous journey guided by the venerable Roman poet Virgil through the nine meticulously descending circles of Hell. The entire structure of this infernal realm is predicated upon the principle of *contrapasso*—a concept mandating that the punishment perfectly and gruesomely counterbalances the sin committed during mortal life. This is not arbitrary cruelty; it is the logical, horrifying extension of one's own transgressions. The sheer intellectual elegance of this design amplifies its terror, for it implies a cosmic order in which suffering is never random but always deserved.

The architectural system of Hell embodies a meticulous, designed order, a stark antithesis to chaos. Its horror resides in its precise, deliberate construction. The structure commences with the lightly punished, those virtuous pagans residing in Limbo, and progressively descends through increasingly severe strata of torment, each layer reserved for those who committed specific Sins of Incontinence, Violence, Fraud, and Treachery. This ordered descent establishes a hierarchy of moral decay, mapping specific vices onto distinct, inescapable environments, proving that every moral lapse has its preordained spatial consequence within the cosmos. The architectural progression is a physical manifestation of a spiritual decline, leading the condemned deeper into both suffering and the immutable logic of divine retribution. The systemic nature denies any possibility of accident or misjudgment; damnation is a calculated destination.

Thematic Anchor: The Mechanics of Contrapasso

The grotesque application of *contrapasso* dictates that, as Dante descends through the infernal architecture, the tortures manifest with an often poetic intensity of cruelty. Schismatics, having divided the Church, are condemned to walk with their bodies literally split open, their wounds a perpetual mirror of their earthly disruption. Flatterers exist eternally mired in filth, their false words transformed into a physical, loathsome abjection. Thieves endure a relentless cycle of being transformed into heaps of ash or fusing grotesquely with terrifying serpents, their very identities stolen and reformed, reflecting their predatory nature. These meticulously designed torments are not random acts of divine wrath; they are the physical embodiments of moral failings, etched onto the very flesh of the damned, each architectural detail of suffering serving a precise retributive function.

The horror is in the unwavering, elegant correspondence between sin and its eternal, visceral consequence. The physical agony is a perfectly crafted didactic tool, a living monument to divine judgment. The culmination of this infernal design resides within the deepest circles, which punish the gravest sins of Treachery. At the frozen core of the ninth circle lies Cocytus, a vast lake of ice where Lucifer resides, not as a chaotic ruler but as a massive, immobile prisoner, eternally chewing upon the ultimate traitors: Judas, Brutus, and Cassius. The greatest horror within this ultimate architectural space is the complete and final fixity and stasis. It is an unchangeable, geometrically perfect prison of suffering, where motion, agency, and hope are utterly extinguished, representing the irrevocable ossification of a soul consumed by betrayal. The freezing static environment signifies a cessation of all natural processes, a permanent, chilling monument to absolute, unalterable damnation.

Thematic Anchor: The Scholastic Blueprint

Dante Alighieri, a Florentine politician, poet, and scholar, witnessed his life tragically interrupted by political upheavals. This profoundly personal context, fused with the intellectual rigor of his era, directly fueled the architecture of dread he constructed. His experiences of betrayal were not external factors; they were the primordial clay from which he molded the theological prison. Dante transformed his intense personal feelings of political and moral injustice into a perfect theological system. The Hell he describes is populated by figures he personally knew, allowing him to enact perfect, divine retribution for the wrongs inflicted upon him. His architecture thus operates on a cosmic scale of absolute justice and a deeply personal canvas of vindication.

The scholastic rigor of Dante's time profoundly influenced the infernal blueprint. Dante wrote during the zenith of Scholasticism, an intellectual movement dedicated to reconciling Classical reason, embodied by Virgil, with Christian faith. The precise, circular, and ordered nature of Hell is a direct reflection of this intellectual discipline. The organization of its concentric circles meticulously follows Aristotle's philosophical classification of sin, establishing that the punishment is mathematical, logical, and inevitable, never arbitrary. This philosophical underpinning renders Hell not merely a place of suffering but a rational, comprehensible system of cosmic law, elevating the horror by making its inexorability a matter of intellect rather than superstition. Dante's work solidified the hegemony of order, elevating popular vision literature into the canonical structure of Hell itself. He provided the indispensable moral law justifying the tortures, imbuing the horror with an intellectual weight that guaranteed its persistence.

Thematic Anchor: The Geometric Prison

Dante's horror mechanics are meticulously crafted, employing precision, geometry, and the profound psychology of finality. His infernal architecture is a masterclass in designing terror through systematic, predictable suffering. The downward tapering structure, descending deeper into the earth, geometrically reflects the intensifying gravity of sin. Each successive circle is a specialized chamber of suffering, designed with mathematical exactitude. This exactitude renders the prison absolute, denying any possibility of escape or reordering. Order itself is the source of horror; it proves definitively that damnation is not a random, chaotic event or a stroke of bad fortune, but a calculated, necessary judgment. This perfect order imbues suffering with a terrifying inevitability. The absolute absence of chaos denies any hope of accidental escape or reprieve; the architectural geometry of Hell makes suffering a foregone conclusion.

Stasis resides at the core of this prison. The final circle, Cocytus, is a vast, frozen lake where the traitors are eternally trapped in ice, unable to move, speak, or interact. This ultimate punishment is the complete denial of all agency and change. The frozen stillness represents the irreversible cessation of life, motion, and even thought. It is a terrifying architectural tableau of absolute fixity, a monument to the soul's ultimate paralysis, where the dynamic torment of earlier circles gives way to the unbearable horror of eternal, unmoving stasis. The geometric precision ensures this stasis is absolute, a perfectly ordered tomb. For sinners such as the thieves, the body is subjected to a constant, painful cycle of destruction and reconstruction. Serpents bite them, their forms consumed by fire, only to be reborn in agony, perpetuating the torture. This continuous, agonizing flux prevents the relief of decay or permanent transformation into nothingness. The body becomes an endlessly renewed vessel for pain, perfectly embodying Pillar B's inescapable physical manifestation of moral rot.

Thematic Anchor: The Lovecraft Metric

Dante's Hell provides a chilling counter-thesis to H.P. Lovecraft's cosmos, illuminating two fundamentally divergent architectures of terror. While both describe vast, systematic, and inescapable structures of dread, Dante's horror is a testament to perfect, divine justice, whereas an absolute, indifferent cosmic void rules Lovecraft's. Lovecraft's environments are cursed because they are metaphysically wrong, governed by alien, incomprehensible laws. Dante's space, Hell itself, is a geometrically perfect prison designed with Scholastic precision to inflict *contrapasso*. The horror resides in the absolute order of the place, which proves the cosmic structure is moral, deliberate, and purposeful, making the suffering intelligible, deserved, and terrifyingly rational. Hell is not alien; it is horrifyingly familiar in its perfect justice.

Lovecraft's cosmic horror often involves a yearning for Uncorporeal Liberation, a desire to shed the "corporeal cage." Dante's body is subjected to the ultimate Eternal Corporeal Cage. Decay and transformation are mechanisms of perpetual punishment. Dante affirms that the soul is bound forever to a physical identity that perfectly embodies its eternal sin. Lovecraft's Conceptual Chaos shatters the mind by proving that the logic of the universe is fundamentally alien. Dante's Logic presents the absolute antithesis of chaos; it embodies perfect conceptual order. The overarching logic is that of perfect justice, which is sound, predictable, and rationally explicable. Lovecraft's cosmos is ultimately unsolvable and indifferent; Dante's Order presents an immense Fantasy of Divine Order. The very existence of Hell proves that the universe cares deeply about human morality; it is profoundly invested in human actions.

Dante Alighieri's *Inferno* represents the high-water mark of the theological age of dread. He assimilated the fragmented proofs and visions of his predecessors—Pliny's curable Law, Gregory's redeemable debt, Tundale's catalogue of visceral tortures—and meticulously refined them into an unassailable, architecturally perfect system. The result was a final, chilling assurance: the punishment for sin was not only mathematically precise, but also eternally fixed and inescapable. He constructed the definitive architectural blueprint for cosmic damnation, a monument to the perfect, unyielding consequence of Pillar B's moral rot. However, the inexorable trajectory of the hegemony demands a fundamental shift. The horror must break free from the constraints of Divine Law and become intrinsically earthly, profoundly human, and paradoxically, curable once more. The geometric prison of Hell must recede, making way for the architectural prison of the ancestral home. The next architect of dread must skillfully transmute the terror of systematic, divine judgment into the pervasive terror of systematic, inherited guilt, establishing a new domestic landscape of psychological torment.

The Evolutionary Handoff: From Divine Decree to Terrestrial Guilt

The completion of Part I marks the formal closure of the **Theological Age of Dread**. Through the architectures of Pliny, Gregory, and William of Malmesbury, we have seen horror function as a rigorous administrative and spiritual system. This movement reached its hegemonic zenith in the work of Dante Alighieri, who provided the ultimate infernal blueprint—a universe of absolute, geometrically perfect justice in which every terror was a precise, inescapable reciprocity for human sin.

The handoff to the next era occurs as the **Fantasy of Divine Order** begins to fracture under the weight of the Enlightenment. As the scientific mind began to dismiss the literal pit of Hell as "superstitious barbarism," the Hegemony was forced to migrate. Dread could no longer rely on the certainty of God's judgment; it required a new, secular vessel.

In the coming chapters, you will witness the **Secularization of the Damned**. The prison of horror moves from the nine circles of the afterlife to the four walls of the ancestral castle. The "Monster" is no longer a demon dispatched by decree, but a **Historical Curse** emerging from the moral rot of a bloodline. The Unbroken Chain now turns its gaze away from the heavens and toward the hearth, inaugurating the age of the **Gothic Rebirth**.

PART II: THE GOTHIC REBIRTH

The Secularization of Dread (1700 – 1850)

Chapter 8: The Enlightenment Gap: Burke and the Graveyard Aesthetic: The Aesthetic of Engineered Dread

The architectural stability of the Theological Age, epitomized by Dante's perfectly ordered Hell, was violently disrupted during the Age of Enlightenment, spanning approximately 1685 to 1815. This era's fervent demand for scientific rationalism and intellectual clarity systematically stripped the supernatural of its serious literary standing, thereby creating a profound and expansive vacuum within the prevailing horror hegemony. The erstwhile terror of God's immutable judgment, once an absolute, was summarily dismissed as "superstitious barbarism." This period does not present a single architect or a singular narrative; rather, it manifests as a confluence of profound philosophical and poetic concepts, meticulously cultivated to sustain the dwindling flame of dread, ultimately providing the intellectual justification for the subsequent Gothic Revival. The critical structural handoff, which directly led to Horace Walpole's architectural endeavors, emerged from the foundational theories of Edmund Burke and the distinctive aesthetic of the Graveyard Poets. This profound shift in the very scaffolding of fear constitutes a pivotal development within Pillar A: The Invasive Breach, addressing the External societal and intellectual realignments that redefined the parameters of dread.

Thematic Anchor: The Burkean Sublime

The Enlightenment Gap stands unequivocally defined by a categorical shift from the horror of Theological Certainty to the horror of Aesthetic Emotion. The supernatural, dislodged from its divine authority, preserved its existence by retreating into the realms of poetry and philosophy, focusing intently upon the *feeling* of terror rather than the factual veracity of damnation. Edmund Burke, a pivotal figure within Pillar C: The Experimental Psyche, presented his 1757 treatise, *A Philosophical Enquiry into the Origin of Our Ideas of the Sublime and Beautiful*, a work that formalized an immutable truth: Terror represents the strongest human emotion, and its most potent evocation proceeds directly from Obscurity, the unknown. This profound declaration granted writers an unprecedented philosophical permission to reintroduce the irrational, as Terror was now designated an aesthetic virtue, a desirable emotional state, rather than a theological vice demanding punishment.

Burke argued with unassailable authority that the sublime—a state of ecstatic awe and profound intellectual transport—was intrinsically and indissolubly linked to terror, thereby positioning terror as the strongest human passion. Crucially, Burke mandated that this sublime terror must be evoked by obscurity and the unknown, concepts that inherently defied rational apprehension. This philosophical mandate provided Horace Walpole with the unequivocal intellectual justification for his irrational, obscure, and fantastic novel, legitimizing a narrative form previously consigned to the intellectual periphery. Burke's intervention did not merely suggest; it ordained the re-entry of the uncanny into serious artistic discourse, creating a conceptual space for dread where none had existed under the dominion of pure reason.

Thematic Anchor: The Graveyard Architecture

Concurrently, the Graveyard Poets, including figures such as Thomas Parnell and Robert Blair, acted as the architects of the genre's necessary scenic backdrop, their collective work firmly rooted in Pillar A, the External realm of physical landscape and mortal observation. They consecrated their verse to themes of mortality, the grandeur of ruins, the solemnity of churchyards, and the inexorable march of decay. These poets meticulously preserved the atmosphere of the macabre, a quality Dante had perfected. Yet, they effected a fundamental substitution: the precise, punitive geometry of Hell was exchanged for the picturesque, melancholic geometry of the tomb.

This intricate interplay between Burke's conceptual framework and the poets' material aesthetics established a new, formidable foundation for dread, relocating its source from divine decree to the intricate mechanisms of human psychological and environmental perception. The architecture of dread in this pivotal period underwent a profound metamorphosis, transitioning from theological accountability to the secular fear of decay and an aesthetic hunger for heightened emotional experience. The Graveyard Poets provided the indispensable aesthetic vocabulary for the nascent Gothic genre. They achieved a critical relocation of the contemplation of mortality, moving it from the abstract theological realm to the concrete, physical, earthly landscape of the cemetery. This group fetishized ruins, tombs, decaying monuments, the spectral light of the moon, and the pervasive quality of shadows as essential elements within their newly constructed landscapes of horror.

Thematic Anchor: The Mechanics of Obscurity

The precise anatomy of terror within the Enlightenment Gap stands defined by its constituent materials: the theoretical framework meticulously laid by Burke and the aesthetic palette supplied by the Graveyard Poets. Burke's mechanics of obscurity furnished the definitive blueprint for the Gothic novel's pervasive atmosphere, a blueprint directly applied in Pillar C. He insisted with absolute conviction that night, profound darkness, and pervasive confusion were crucial elements for generating terror because these conditions systematically prevent the rational mind from fully processing or comprehending the true nature of the perceived danger. The archetypal Gothic castle, with its labyrinthine dark corridors and hidden chambers, stands as a direct structural application of Burke's fundamental principle.

Moreover, Burke posited that terror inherently associates with entities of vastness, such as the unfathomable sea, and with forces possessing irresistible power, beyond human control or comprehension. This philosophical axiom rigorously justified the Gothic's consistent utilization of massive, oppressive architecture and the introduction of uncontrollable supernatural forces. The Graveyard Poets supplied the literal "props" for this new literary dread, engaging directly with Pillar A. Unlike Dante's body, which remained fixed in perpetual contrapasso as a symbol of divine justice, the body in the Graveyard aesthetic is simply decaying matter, destined for worms and dust. The horror returns to the primordial fear of mortality itself, stripped of theological purpose. The focus centers squarely upon the worm, the dust, and the skeletal remains—the undeniable, physical evidence of dissolution. These poets also mastered the strategic deployment of melancholy, introducing a fundamentally new pace of dread: slow, deliberate, and contemplative.

Thematic Anchor: The Lovecraft Metric

This chapter vividly demonstrates the dramatic shift in hegemony away from Dante's fixed theological system and decisively toward a secular philosophical basis that would ultimately inform Lovecraft's unique brand of horror. The environmental horror, which, in Dante's construction, represented a perfect, rational, and moral Hell, finds a profound reinterpretation here. The environment becomes primarily Aesthetic and Poetic, a landscape of evocative decay. The scenery of churchyards and ruins systematically removes the moral justification for the horror; dread is divorced from divine judgment. This serves as a necessary precursor to Lovecraft's later works, which would similarly excise the moral justification for dread while rigorously retaining the powerful aesthetic elements of vastness and pervasive gloom.

The ecstasy of decay, concerning the body, shifts from Dante's eternally fixed contrapasso to the Graveyard Body, which is simply dust and worms. The terror becomes stripped of theological purpose, reverting to the fundamental fear of inevitable mortality. This secular approach to corporeal decay paved an inescapable path for the biological horror of Lovecraft, where the human body stands revealed as a fragile and ultimately insignificant shell. Conceptual chaos, which in Dante's Hell was defined by perfect conceptual order, finds its justification in Burke's logic. Burke's philosophy justifies aesthetic irrationality, mandating that terror achieves its greatest strength when the danger remains Obscure. This constitutes the necessary philosophical predecessor to Lovecraft's anti-rational logic; Lovecraft's non-Euclidean geometry finds its conceptual lineage in this very Burkean principle. The Gothic demand replaces Divine Law with a Historical Curse. This persistent, unquantifiable dread, rooted in the inexorable past, fundamentally aligns with Pillar B: The Symmetrical Debt, the Moral Rot that permeates the fabric of inherited legacies, ultimately leading to a pervasive sense of doom.

The Enlightenment Gap, meticulously navigated by the philosophical and aesthetic innovations of this period, conclusively establishes that the profound death of theological certainty absolutely necessitated the invention of a new, secular aesthetic of terror. This constitutes a monumental undertaking within Pillar C, for it involved the deliberate engineering of human emotional response. The Graveyard Poets provided the tangible materials—the ruins, the tombs, the melancholy landscapes—for this burgeoning dread. Edmund Burke provided the indispensable philosophical imprimatur to reintroduce the irrational, embracing Obscurity and the Sublime as legitimate sources of profound human experience. The hegemony now transitions directly into the hands of the first truly self-aware architect of the modern horror era, Horace Walpole. He skillfully synthesized these disparate components into a cohesive narrative structure, thereby creating the inaugural novel that intentionally invoked the specific Burkean form of terror. This foundational shift replaces Dante's absolute, theological judgment with the complex, secular problem of Inherited Guilt, making the castle the new, confining, and psychologically resonant architecture of dread. The Gothic Age is unequivocally born.

Chapter 9 Horace Walpole: The Architecture of Inherited Dread

The dominion of Dante's meticulously ordered theological cosmos and the subsequent demand for scientific rationalism, which emerged from the Enlightenment's crucible, together forged an undeniable crisis for the very possibility of narrative horror; within such an intellectual paradigm, the supernatural was systematically discredited. It was Horace Walpole (1717–1797), an architect of fiction and culture, who consciously and deliberately rejected this severe intellectual constraint, thereby returning the visceral power of terror to the literary hegemony. His seminal novel, *The Castle of Otranto*, published in 1764, stands as the singular, genre-defining pivot in this profound shift, establishing the Gothic Turn irrevocably; it systematically dismantled the geometric certainty of Hell as a fixed consequence for individual sin, replacing it with the chaotic, haunting architecture of inherited, earthly guilt. This profound reorientation of dread shifts its focus from the punitive suffering inflicted for individual transgression to the inescapable, tragic burden of history itself, a weight pressing down through generations, inescapable and absolute. The narrative reveals not a divine reckoning but a historical one, wherein the very stones of the past conspire against the present. This establishes the foundation of horror as rooted in

Pillar B: The Symmetrical Debt, the inexorable weight of Moral Rot.

Thematic Anchor: The Architecture of Dread

A profound disquiet settled upon the rationalist spirit of the 18th century, a longing for the wildness of an older world, a sensibility Walpole, a wealthy art historian and politician, held as sacred. He possessed an unwavering enthusiasm for the past's aesthetic and philosophical principles, notably those articulated by Edmund Burke, which posited terror as a source of the Sublime. Walpole's creation of Otranto was a conscious, deliberate endeavor to synthesize the unrestrained, imaginative "wildness" inherent in ancient romances with the rigorous demands for psychological depth prevalent in the modern novel. This blending was a deliberate act of intellectual fusion, forging a new narrative alloy. The novel unfolds within a massive, anachronistic castle in Italy, a structure deliberately conceived as an oppressive stage where the tyrannical Prince Manfred harbors an absolute obsession with securing the perpetuity of his dynasty. This fortress, ancient and brooding, is not merely a setting; it is a repository of generational malfeasance, its very stones imbued with an oppressive history.

An ancient prophecy triggers the central horror of the narrative: a decree whispered through time that states, with immutable finality, "The castle and lordship of Otranto should pass from the present family, whenever the real owner should be grown too large to inhabit it." The supernatural attack occurs in the opening moments, a spectacle of impossible scale: Manfred's only son, Conrad, is annihilated by a gigantic helmet that plummets from the sky, a spectacle of impossible scale and irrational violence. This fantastic event stands in absolute opposition to the calculated, systematic justice of Dante's theological order, where every punishment possesses a clear moral antecedent. Here, the horror is immediate, disorienting, and without a rational precursor. The castle's spectral haunting intensifies with statues that bleed, portraits that sigh, and the appearance of the giant apparition of the rightful ancestor, Alfonso. The narrative's resolution arrives with cataclysmic finality: the castle's walls collapse, a physical manifestation of the curse's release. The horror finds its absolute cessation only when the historical curse is fulfilled and the rightful heir, Theodore, is at last revealed.

Thematic Anchor: The Strawberry Hill Manifesto

Horace Walpole's distinct context as an eccentric aristocrat, profoundly obsessed with the vestiges of the past and the subjective experience of emotion, forms the fundamental intellectual bedrock of the Gothic genre itself. He was not a mere chronicler, but an architect of new narrative sensibilities. Walpole actively, even defiantly, rejected the scientific determinism and the architectural strictness that defined his age. His personal creative act, the construction of his own residence, Strawberry Hill, stands as an architectural manifesto. This edifice was conceived in an eccentric, self-consciously "Gothic" style, a deliberate pastiche that eschewed contemporary rational design for a fantastical, intricate, and deeply personal aesthetic of antiquity.

This house served as a literal, three-dimensional laboratory for the aesthetics of gloom, decay, and the picturesque, embodying the subjective mood over objective utility. *The Castle of Otranto*, then, became the literary translation of this strange, irrational architecture, a textual edifice mirroring the physical one; it is a clear manifestation of Pillar C: The Experimental Psyche, manifesting directly in structural design. Walpole's aesthetic choices were not arbitrary; he sought to evoke the highest aesthetic sensation: Sublime Terror, the profound disquiet caused by vastness, obscurity, and power. His novel was initially published under a pseudonym and presented as a genuine translation of a medieval Italian manuscript. This intentional deception, the now-canonical "found manuscript" trope, served as his strategic method for side-stepping the inevitable rational critique from an audience conditioned to demand verisimilitude. It was a deliberate intellectual maneuver, a mask. The horror depicted in

Otranto is consciously irrational—consider the giant helmet's descent or the weeping statues. This calculated irrationality presented a direct challenge to the Enlightenment's pervasive demand for logical causality.

Thematic Anchor: Inherited Guilt and Dynastic Collapse

Walpole effected a profound and indelible shift, moving the architecture of dread from theological fear of divine retribution to the secular, politically charged fear of illegitimacy and dynastic collapse. This was a move from the eternal to the temporal. The castle functions as the immutable foundation of this new, secular dread; it is a confining, oppressive, and inherited prison. This medieval architecture literally holds the historical secrets, particularly the foundational murder of the rightful ancestor, Alfonso, which invariably contaminates the present. The profound horror lies in the absolute realization that the past is not a dead, distant entity, but an active, malevolent force that relentlessly haunts the living, demanding reckoning. The anxiety shifts demonstrably from individual Sin to a pervasive, inescapable Inherited Guilt.

Manfred's torment is not born of his own choices alone, but represents a karmic debt for the original sin of his grandfather. This usurper now seeks its immutable justice through a series of escalating supernatural events. The Gothic genre established an absolute rule: the modern protagonist is cursed by the indelible crimes of their distant ancestors, demonstrating a pervasive Moral Rot woven into the fabric of lineage. Manfred is presented as the ultimate tyrant: violent and absolutely willing to violate all laws to maintain his usurped power. He embodies the dangerous excesses of unchecked aristocratic authority. The narrative's resolution satisfies a profound cultural need for justice and the restoration of legitimate social order. The supernatural functions as the irrefutable mechanism by which the divine right of ancestors is enforced, acting as a cosmic corrective against corrupt and illegitimate modern power, thereby addressing Pillar A: The Invasive Breach societal anxieties through fantastical means.

Thematic Anchor: The Anatomy of Terror

Walpole's horror mechanics are meticulously constructed on the Burkean sublime, the unsettling power of the fragmented body, and the absolute failure of human reason to adequately account for the overwhelming spectacle. The mechanics of the Sublime Spectacle were directly informed by Burke's instructions, compelling Walpole to achieve terror through the deployment of irrational, overwhelming objects that defy easy comprehension. The opening horror is predicated upon a massive, supernatural fragmentation of the body: Conrad is crushed by an impossibly giant helmet. This is followed by a persistent haunting by fragments of the ancestor

Alfonso: a colossal leg appearing on a staircase and an immense disembodied hand. These impossible, disproportionate objects overwhelm the characters' senses, achieving the Burkean Sublime through sheer Vastness and Obscurity.

The fragment becomes terrifying precisely because it implies the immense, unknowable scale of the whole. The architecture itself, the castle, moves, sighs, and ultimately collapses, thus proving incontrovertibly that the material structures of the world hold the absolute key to the curse, acting as physical conduits for historical vengeance. This is the castle becoming an active, sentient agent of dread. Walpole intentionally employs architecture to cultivate a pervasive sense of psychological and physical disorientation, a deliberate failure of rational space. The entire narrative unfolds within the oppressive confines of the castle, a deliberate choice that generates a persistent sense of Claustrophobia. The labyrinthine pursuit of Isabella through subterranean vaults transforms the architecture into the primary antagonist. No character possesses the capacity to process the unfolding events rationally; they are instead driven entirely by overwhelming fear and an escalating sense of dread, demonstrating the triumph of emotion over intellect. Despite the profound irrationality of the events, the curse itself is, fundamentally, solvable. Walpole masterfully combines the visceral dread of the supernatural with the solvable, almost juridical, structure of Pliny's Juridical Specter, offering a narrative closure that distinguishes it from later, more nihilistic forms.

Thematic Anchor: The Lovecraft Metric

Walpole's Gothic Turn stands as the necessary and absolute transition point that inaugurates the secular tradition of horror. It irrevocably establishes an aesthetic framework that H.P. Lovecraft would later adopt with profound reverence, yet simultaneously and vehemently reject its underlying moral cosmology. In terms of environmental horror, Walpole's castle is a confined, earthly, Cursed Space. The dread it emanates stems from environmental contamination, but the contaminant is the corrosive residue of human history and human guilt. This crucial secularization of the cursed space proves essential for Lovecraft, whose later Cursed House, while saturated with alien historical contamination, remains utterly devoid of inherent moral weight.

In the ecstasy of decay, Walpole's fragmented body serves as a material manifestation of the curse. The sight of Alfonso's giant, fragmented remains achieves Burke's Sublime through its overwhelming scale. This focus on the body as a fragmented, unnatural spectacle constitutes a decisive step toward Lovecraft's later fascination with alien biology and grotesque corporeal distortion. Regarding conceptual chaos, Walpole deliberately injects irrational chaos—the inexplicable fall of the giant helmet—into the Enlightenment's meticulously ordered world. This engineered absurdity is explicitly justified by Burke's philosophy, which posits that Obscurity and the Irrational are necessary components for the experience of the Sublime. Walpole's audacious act provides the first, self-aware literary permission slip for the kind of anti-rational, non-Euclidean logic that Lovecraft later perfected. Finally, the fantasy of order: Walpole's curse is ultimately solvable and profoundly moral. The Gothic novel's fundamental fantasy is that history, however dark or oppressive, can ultimately be corrected. This provides a narrative comfort that Lovecraft aggressively denied; Walpole's world remains meaningful and, ultimately, just.

Walpole's *The Castle of Otranto* marks a decisive and absolute shift from the theological paradigm of dread to a distinctly secular aesthetic of terror. He successfully replaced Dante's philosophical Hell with the earthly, confining Architecture of Inherited Guilt. This structural innovation pivoted horror from the cosmic to the familial, from the eternal to the historical. His intentional blend of the rational and the irrational established the foundational structural framework for the horror literature of the subsequent two centuries. This framework, now established, demands refinement. Walpole's basic structure, while groundbreaking, requires expansion into more nuanced and distinct literary modes: specifically, the slow, pervasive psychological suspense. The next structural architect in the hegemony of dread must therefore take Walpole's architectural setting—the ancient, cursed castle—and transform it into a confining stage for protracted, internal psychological torment. The genre, having established external, historical haunting, now demands a master who can prove that the most terrifying phantoms are those conjured by the heroine's own fractured mind, a transition from the External to the Internal.

Chapter 10 Ann Radcliffe: The Chimeric Edifice of the Explained Supernatural

The human mind, in its most confined and vulnerable state, possesses a singular capacity to conjure specters of its own undoing; this inherent psychological architecture forms the foundational truth of dread, a reality Ann Radcliffe (1764–1823) profoundly illuminates. Horace Walpole (Chapter 8) provided the initial blueprint for the Gothic genre, establishing the architectural stage of the isolated castle and inscribing upon its stones the problem of Inherited Guilt, a tangible, external burden. Radcliffe, with an almost surgical precision, introduced the psychological mechanism, converting Walpole's static scaffold of dread into a dynamic, internal crucible. Her seminal works, particularly *The Mysteries of Udolpho* (1794), perfected the Female Gothic, meticulously defining terror not through the vulgar, visceral spectacle of demons, but through the slow, sustained, and insidious torture inflicted upon the heroine's acutely perceptive mind. This profound transformation of the horror landscape, pivoting from the external to the internal, firmly anchors Radcliffe's work within Pillar C: The Experimental Psyche, exploring the ultimate limits of human psychological endurance.

Thematic Anchor: The Psychology of Confinement

The thematic anchor of Radcliffe's oeuvre resides in the deliberate transition from external spectacle to the immersive realm of internal suspense. Her primary narrative subject is invariably the vulnerable, acutely perceptive heroine, systematically subjected to the debilitating forces of isolation and the pervasive threat of male tyranny. The confined heroine represents the experimental subject in this psychological architecture of dread, her consciousness a sensorium for manufactured terror. *The Mysteries of Udolpho* centers on Emily St. Aubert, whose very existence becomes a protracted ordeal of incarceration under the cruel guardianship of Montoni within the formidable, isolated bastion of Udolpho Castle. This colossal structure ceases to be a mere setting; it transmutes into the perfect psychological prison, its vastness and isolation pressing in upon Emily's consciousness.

The mechanism of suspense, the very engine of Radcliffean dread, is constructed through intense, prolonged psychological pressure. Emily endures a ceaseless barrage of mysterious sounds, fleeting shadows, and tantalizingly veiled horrors—spectral moans that echo in desolate corridors and secret passages, hinting at unseen machinations. The narrative, with deliberate precision, delays the revelation of these secrets for hundreds of pages, a masterful manipulation that compels the reader to inhabit the heroine's protracted psychological torment. The resolution of reason, Radcliffe's defining structural device, is the Explained Supernatural. In the final chapters, every ghostly event is revealed to possess a rational, earthly cause. This systematic reduction of the ghost to human agency constitutes an architectural triumph; it irrefutably proves that psychological terror, born of human machinations and interpreted by a susceptible mind, represents the most potent and enduring form of dread.

Thematic Anchor: The Female Gothic and Pillar B

Ann Radcliffe composed her definitive works at the height of the Gothic craze, the 1790s, a tumultuous era scarred by the French Revolution and by rampant societal anxiety over political upheaval. Her personal context inextricably informed her decision to elevate confinement and female vulnerability as central themes of the genre. This period fueled a pervasive popular anxiety regarding the complete dissolution of social order and exposed the inherent dangers of unchecked male power, manifesting as Pillar B: Moral Rot. Radcliffe's output established the Female Gothic as a dominant literary form. The narrative architecture revolves around a passive heroine subjected to systematic confinement and relentless persecution by a tyrannical male figure, such as Montoni.

This narrative paradigm reflects the real-world vulnerability of women in the 18th century, a period characterized by their profound lack of legal autonomy, making the domestic sphere a site of terror. Radcliffe was a profound product of the late Enlightenment; her commitment to the Explained Supernatural was a philosophical necessity. She satisfied the reader's emotional desire for terror while respecting the era's intellectual demand for a rational conclusion. She demonstrated that true artistic mastery lay in the sophisticated mastery of psychological suspense. Radcliffe refined Walpole's framework by forging a chronic anxiety, an internal gnawing dread. She imparted the truth that terror attains its greatest potency when it remains delayed, internal, and perpetually ambiguous. The fear originates in the realm of what might be, in the terrifying possibility of the supernatural, rather than in its confirmed, explicit occurrence.

Thematic Anchor: The Veil of Obscurity

Radcliffe's cultural architecture of dread establishes a profound reliance upon the societal fear of isolation and the inherently subjective nature of human reality. The castle of Udolpho stands as a monumental symbol of unfettered male tyranny, its imposing walls embodying the patriarch's absolute power. The macabre of self-doubt, a terrifying internal shift, emerges from Radcliffe's rational resolution. By explaining away the ghostly, Radcliffe compels the horror to migrate from the external specter to the heroine's own mind. The dread becomes rooted in the chilling realization that the heroine's extreme fear was the true progenitor of the phantoms she perceived. This revelation introduces a horrifying new dimension: the fear that the victim is succumbing to madness, a direct assault on the integrity of her own consciousness.

Radcliffe articulated a critical distinction between Terror—an intellectual suspense preceding the object's full revelation—and Horror—the disgusting, visceral shock unleashed once the object is definitively seen. She meticulously employs the principle of Obscurity, as mandated by Burke, to retain the object of fear in an indeterminate state for the longest possible duration. The narrative mechanism of the veil constitutes her central device—the deliberate obfuscation of the object of fear. The act of lifting the veil represents the narrative's climax of terror, yet the subsequent rational explanation provides the intellectual resolution. The most infamous veiled corpse is ultimately revealed as a mere wax effigy, an empty signifier, proving the power of suggestion over substance. This conditions the reader to fear the potential rather than the concrete reality.

Thematic Anchor: The Lovecraft Metric

Radcliffe's horror, though rigorously secular, is fundamentally moralistic and psychological, establishing its distinct distance from the nihilistic cosmicism of Lovecraft. Her unwavering commitment to solvable rationalism stands in direct and absolute contrast to Lovecraft's mandate for the unknowable, unsolvable void. Lovecraft's environmental horror presents spaces ruled by alien laws; Radcliffe's castle, Udolpho, functions as a Human-Contaminated Space. Its curse originates solely from human cruelty—Montoni's tyranny—not from any inherent cosmic malevolence. This space is demonstrably purifiable once the human villain is removed, a direct inverse of Lovecraft's cursed places, which cannot be redeemed.

The ecstasy of decay finds no resonance in Radcliffe. Her veiled corpse is treated as a mere prop in a psychological drama. The wax effigy symbolizes a deliberate denial of a real, decayed body, ensuring the horror remains entirely subjective and manageable. While Lovecraft's conceptual chaos shatters the human mind with alien logic, Radcliffe's rationalism presents a world ultimately governed by perfect rational order. The terror in her narratives is predicated upon a temporary confusion of facts, not a fundamental structural collapse of reality itself. Lovecraft's cosmos is unsolvable and hostile, offering no solace. Radcliffe's solvable psychology provides a profound Fantasy of Order. The heroine and the reader are ultimately rewarded with a world where reason triumphs, wickedness is justly punished, and the natural world is restored to equilibrium. The terror is thus managed, a sublime thrill, not an existential threat.

Ann Radcliffe completed the first major refinement of the Gothic genre, transforming the foundational castle into a confining stage specifically designed for protracted psychological suspense. Her commitment to the Explained Supernatural unequivocally demonstrated the immense power of the human mind to generate its own terrifying dread. However, this systematic demystification inadvertently rendered the genre safe and polite, contained within the strictures of reason. This containment proved unsustainable for the hegemony of horror. The genre now demands a violent rejection of this intellectual containment. The structural legacy of this chapter is the creation of an immense void, compelling the next structural architect to dismiss the very need for rational explanation and to revive the raw, visceral, and genuinely demonic horror that Radcliffe so studiously averted. The era demands the return of the explicit and the unforgivable into the evolving Gothic novel, a rebellion against the confines of reason.

Chapter 11 Matthew Lewis: The Grand Basilica of Abject Depravity

The aesthetic of Terror, meticulously refined by Ann Radcliffe, established a landscape of subtle psychological dread, a realm where rational explanation ultimately offered curative absolution. This cultivated restraint, however, created a profound structural vacuum within the prevailing literary hegemony, conspicuously denying readers the raw, explicit confrontation with evil that Medieval texts, such as Dante's *Inferno*, had unequivocally promised. Matthew Gregory Lewis (1775–1818), acting as a necessary counter-reaction, delivered a brutal architectural intervention. His pivotal novel, *The Monk* (1796), violently rejected Radcliffe's cultivated politeness, shattering the illusion of remediable fear. Lewis codified the Horror Gothic, resurrecting the unforgiving theological certainty of damnation and visceral spectacle; he placed this primordial darkness into a modern context defined by sexual depravity, institutional corruption, and supernatural reality. This project constitutes a critical expansion of Pillar B: The Symmetrical Debt, introducing Moral Rot as an inherent, inescapable feature of human and institutional existence.

Thematic Anchor: The Fall from Grace

Lewis's novel delineates the precipitous decline of Ambrosio, the revered Capuchin monk, celebrated across

Madrid for his profound sanctity. This narrative swiftly descends into total, unstoppable depravity, a meticulously observed dismantling of moral fortitude. The Fall from Grace initiates with Matilda, a noblewoman cloaked as the monk Rosario, whose seductive machinations awaken a fierce, long-repressed lust within Ambrosio. This initial transgression does not remain contained; it unfurls as a cancerous growth upon his soul. His desires intensify without natural limit, shifting irrevocably toward the innocent virgin Antonia. Ambrosio, now corrupted, employs black magic—facilitated by Matilda, who reveals herself as an overt agent of Satan—to rape and murder Antonia within the monastery crypts.

This act stands as a definitive profanation, sealing his fate. The Climax and Damnation arrive with Ambrosio's seizure by the Inquisition, a transient earthly judgment from which he escapes the pyre by selling his soul to the Devil. This infernal pact, however, is a mere prelude to ultimate horror: the Devil reveals Antonia's identity as Ambrosio's long-lost sister, confirming his commission of both incest and matricide. The Devil then irrevocably breaches the contract, precluding any possibility of repentance, and casts Ambrosio's soul into Hell via a prolonged, torturous death upon a precipice. The horror is absolute; it remains unforgivable. This detailed mapping of spiritual catastrophe is a foundational expansion of Pillar B, outlining the insidious mechanisms of Moral Rot.

Thematic Anchor: The Experimental Psyche of Infamy

Matthew Lewis simultaneously courted intense controversy; this duality found its precise mirroring in the scandalous content of his debut novel. His infamy as "Monk" Lewis commenced when *The Monk*, penned in a mere ten weeks, appeared anonymously and ignited an immediate sensation due to its unvarnished, explicit content. The subsequent revelation of his identity precipitated a severe backlash; critics condemned the work as "immoral" and "obscene." Lewis faced undeniable public pressure and was compelled to issue an expurgated edition to safeguard his seat in the House of Commons. This represents a clear manifestation of Pillar C: The Experimental Psyche, showcasing a mind that willfully provoked the established moral order.

The anti-Catholic backdrop of the novel directly exploited the rampant English anti-Catholicism of the era. Lewis masterfully utilized the perceived rigidity and secrecy of Catholic institutions—monasteries and convents—as a metaphorical breeding ground for vice. This strategic deployment of existing societal anxieties is a direct engagement with Pillar A: The Invasive Breach, leveraging external cultural currents to amplify the novel's shock value. Lewis explicitly posits that the monastic system, designed for virtue, instead "rooted out his virtues, and... allowed every vice... to arrive at full perfection." He suggests that organized religion becomes the very mechanism through which Gothic monsters are made. This profound indictment of institutional corruption firmly entrenches the narrative within Pillar B, defining Moral Rot as a systemic rather than individual failing.

Thematic Anchor: Subversion of Sacred Space

Lewis's architecture of dread is defined by the profound moral corruption of sacred institutions and the absolute return of the explicit, visceral horror that Radcliffe had assiduously avoided. The subversion of sacred space is a central structural pillar of Lewis's design; he transforms the conventional Gothic setting into the very locus of the most profound spiritual depravity. The Convent of Saint Clare is depicted as an institution that actively embodies hypocrisy and repression. The monastery crypts, with their clandestine tunnels, evolve from places of quiet sanctity to the precise sites where repressed sexuality and perversion thrive, festering unchecked beneath a fragile facade of piety.

Violence as currency permeates the novel's narrative, establishing explicit brutality as a measure of power. The cruelty inflicted upon the female body—the protracted torture of Agnes, the brutal rape of Antonia—is not gratuitous; it stands as the horrific, inevitable consequence of unchecked institutional authority. This unflinching realism of violence unequivocally separates Lewis's work from Radcliffe's more suggestive atmosphere. Lewis directly rejects the Explained Supernatural, reinstating the absolute, unforgiving power of the demonic. The Devil and his agents are literal, active, and malevolent forces. This reassertion of genuine supernatural evil re-establishes a pre-Enlightenment cosmic order. The horror of incest and matricide revived the severe, systematic moral accounting of the Medieval Age, reaffirming the existence of absolute, cosmic moral laws and their terrifying consequences.

Thematic Anchor: The Anatomy of Terror

Lewis's anatomy of terror is constructed upon psychological collapse, the transgressive fusion of the erotic and the horrific, and the visceral spectacle of the corruptible body. Lewis utilizes Ambrosio's celebrated piety to maximize the devastating impact of his fall. This detailed charting of internal erosion is a masterful deployment of Pillar C. The grotesque climax unfolds in the abbey's crypts, spaces already imbued with the scent of mortality and decay. These subterranean chambers, filled with the rotting bodies of the deceased, become the stage for rape and murder, a synthesis of *Eros* and *Thanatos*. This fusion is a crucial, transgressive step that Lewis introduces to the horror hegemony, dismantling traditional boundaries of decorum.

The mechanism of ultimate damnation Lewis crafts in his final scenes is a systematic denial of hopeful resolutions. The Devil actively prevents Ambrosio's last-minute repentance, ensuring his fate is irreversible. This is not an act of chance; it is a precise, theological execution. The subsequent five-day, prolonged death upon the rocky precipice serves as the secular equivalent of Dante's geometrically precise Hell. This absolute denial of redemption and the explicit, prolonged suffering solidify a new paradigm of terror, firmly rooted in Pillar A's external, unyielding cosmic justice. The fragmented body of Ambrosio during his final fall is not merely a grotesque destruction; it is a profoundly purposeful act. The body itself becomes dominated by violence and pain, serving as a "currency of power," a tangible manifestation of cosmic retribution.

Thematic Anchor: The Lovecraft Metric

Lewis's *The Monk* stands at a conceptual antipode to Lovecraft's indifference, for it asserts an intensely concerned universe. Yet, its visceral, explicit horror provides foundational aesthetic stepping stones. Lewis's sacred spaces are systematically contaminated, transformed into Contaminated Sacred Spaces. This internal rot confirms a core Lovecraftian aesthetic: the potent belief that established institutions and places of supposed safety can be utterly destabilized and corrupted. The ecstasy of decay finds a brutal counterpoint in Lewis's work. Lewis affirms the body as the absolute site of visceral, physical, and sexual trauma. The body is not something to be transcended; it is the unwilling vessel of judgment.

Lewis unequivocally rejects Radcliffe's rationally ordered universe, reasserting a terrible, unforgiving theological order. However, he simultaneously destabilizes human institutions, creating a world in which there is, paradoxically, no universal rational and moral order that humanity can reliably depend on. This profound tension aligns with Lovecraft's worldview, in which human order proves fragile before an indifferent or malevolent cosmos. The fantasy of order is utterly dismantled by Lewis, anticipating Lovecraft's unsolvable and indifferent cosmos. In Lewis's narrative, the ultimate reality is annihilation. The conclusion is guaranteed damnation and irreversible judgment. This decisive, final ending rejects the comforting moral restoration characteristic of Walpole and Radcliffe, forging a form of absolute, secularized theological horror.

Matthew Lewis definitively completed the necessary bifurcation of the Gothic genre. By prioritizing Horror over Terror, he violently ruptured the psychological containment established by Radcliffe, thereby resurrecting the powerful, unforgivable supernatural reality characteristic of the Medieval

Age. His explicit use of sex, violence, and institutional corruption injected a potent, new, and visceral energy into the hegemony, proving that horror could be both explicit and uncompromising. The structural legacy of Lewis is profound; he created a genre fundamentally split between the psychological and the visceral. However, the Hegemony now demanded a pivot toward the emerging horrors of the New World. The time was irrevocably ripe for the Gothic to transcend the walls of the monastery and address the ultimate anxiety of the nineteenth century: the cold, mathematical reality of human property. The next architect must take the inherited guilt of the Gothic and the fragmented, suffering body of Lewis's victims and transplant them into a landscape where the "Demon" is not a fallen monk, but a ratified Legal Code. The stage was now set for Victor Séjour.

Chapter 12 Victor Séjour: The Blueprint of Inevitable Atrocity

The innate corruption of man finds its ultimate expression not in individual depravity but in collective, sanctioned atrocity. Matthew Gregory Lewis, in his Gothic edifices, unveiled the horrors of monastic corruption, in which human frailties festered into carnal transgressions, confining the source of evil to the moral decay of the individual soul. His horrors, though visceral, remained tethered to the specter of divine judgment and supernatural intervention. This narrative architecture could not encompass the burgeoning, systematic malevolence that arose with the transatlantic exchange of human beings, a new form of damnation forged not in Hell's fire but in the crucible of commerce and chattel. The very concept of humanity underwent a brutal redefinition under the merciless hand of nascent capitalism. Thus, the intellectual hegemony required a structural evolution, a radical re-anchoring of dread that transitioned from theological to legislative, from the supernatural to the profoundly systemic. Victor Séjour, a pivotal architect of this secular damnation, meticulously codified this shift. His seminal short story, *Le Mulâtre* (1837), deliberately excoriated the Gothic's supernatural safety net. It transferred the genre's inherent visceral energy into the unyielding, omnipresent Systemic Trap of American slavery. Séjour demonstrated that the Law constituted a more terrifying entity than any Devil, and the Plantation served as a more efficient and inescapable site of damnation than any ancient abbey. This foundational shift established a crucial new wing upon the house of horror, rooting its terrors firmly within Pillar A: The Invasive Breach, where the machinery of oppression operated with bureaucratic efficiency.

Thematic Anchor: The Systemic Trap

The illusion of agency proves a fatal conceit within the Systemic Trap, a structure designed to crush the individual spirit under the weight of predetermined roles. Séjour's narrative, the earliest known work of African American fiction, centers on Georges, an enslaved man on a Saint-Domingue plantation, whose very existence is defined by his status as property. Georges operates under a profound "Fantasy of Order," believing that his loyalty and demonstrated merit—twice preserving his master Alfred's life—could transcend the absolute condition of his chattel status. This belief in an inherent, transactional justice is a cruel deception, a psychological construct built only to be systematically demolished. The true structural reality of the plantation, a "Systemic Breach," is violently revealed when Alfred's unrestrained lust compels him to pursue Zélie, Georges's wife.

Her resistance is met with a swift, brutal execution, an act sanctioned by the very master Georges protected, proving allegiance holds no currency against absolute ownership and the perverse logic of the system. The climax of this horror is not an emotional outburst but a cold, deterministic vengeance. Driven to an act of retribution, Georges murders Alfred, an act that seems to reclaim a fragment of agency. Yet this transgression is immediately inverted. In the final, visceral moments, Alfred's wife reveals the "Gothic Truth": Alfred was Georges's biological father, making the murder an act of parricide, a crime engineered by the system itself. This revelation seals Georges's fate; realizing the profound, biological transgression forced upon him by the very structures of power, he commits suicide. The horror is absolute; the system has orchestrated a scenario where the victim is forced into the role of ultimate transgressor. This establishes the profound impact of Pillar B: The Symmetrical Debt, as the system's Moral Rot corrodes kinship and identity.

Thematic Anchor: The Double Consciousness of the Architect

The architect of this new dread inhabited a liminal space, granting him a peculiar clarity regarding the American experiment's inherent contradictions. Victor Séjour's existence spanned the rigid racial castes of New Orleans and the radical intellectual milieu of Paris, a "Double Consciousness" that afforded him an unparalleled perspective. Born a "free man of color" in New Orleans, he was a direct witness to the "Legal Ghost" status of his peers, individuals legally distinct yet socially bound by the strictures of chattel slavery. His transplantation to Paris in 1836 enabled him to audit the American Gothic from a position of relative safety, transforming personal trauma into a clinical analysis of power. Educated among the "Cercle des Philadelphes," a group of Black intellectuals, Séjour weaponized the Gothic genre as a trenchant political tool.

He discerned that the true "Monsters" of the American South possessed no supernatural origin; they were legislative entities, codified in law and enforced by brutal custom. Séjour lived the horrifying paradox in which a human could be simultaneously a biological "son" and a mere "movable property." This duality forms the "Source Code" of his horror: the absolute realization that the Law possessed the power to redact biological fact, rendering kinship null before the altar of commerce. This biographical context is essential to understanding the influence of Pillar A, the External forces of legal oppression, on his artistic output. The transition from inherited moral decay to systemic malice redefined the geometry of terror. Séjour's architecture meticulously subverts the plantation's pastoral facade, transforming the "Great House" from a symbol of prosperity into a crucible of predation. The plantation is revealed not as an agrarian enterprise but as a "Clockwork Nightmare," its gears designed to extract labor and obliterate identity.

Thematic Anchor: The Civil Code as Black Magic

Where Matthew Gregory Lewis presented the Devil as the reliable antagonist, Séjour posits the Civil Code as the true infernal power. The Law becomes the "Black Magic" itself, granting a father the legal right to sell or execute his own son, an atrocity sanctioned by the documents meant to define civil order. Séjour vehemently rejects the "Explained Supernatural," dismissing the presence of ghouls. His horror is "Explained Systemic," asserting that no phantom lurks in the attic; only a binding contract resides in the courthouse, a document dictating suffering. The "Biological Trap" within this system, culminating in parricide, demonstrates the plantation's "Closed Loop" design, which ensnares its victims in a moral labyrinth. Their every exit is barred by their own blood, a testament to the inherent corruption of Pillar B that defines the system itself.

Séjour's Anatomy of Terror dissects the human condition under legal tyranny, revealing the mutilation of identity. The psychological eradication of Georges defines his terror; his true horror is the condition of "Social Death." His "piety" toward his master functions as a psychological defense mechanism that the system eventually shatters. The grotesque recognition, the "Oedipal Pivot," occurs not as a moment of salvation but as a final damnation. In traditional Gothic narratives, the "lost son" receives recognition; Séjour's "Systemic Gothic" inverts this, revealing the truth of paternity only after the blood of parricide has been spilled. This fusion of familial bonds with terminal violence irrevocably integrates the Black experience into the Gothic hegemony. The mechanism of finality is absolute. No "Inquisition" exists to arrest the Master, for the Master embodies the Inquisition itself. This creates a vacuum of justice, leaving self-destruction as the sole outcome.

Thematic Anchor: The Lovecraft Metric

Séjour's narrative presages a more cosmic indifference, articulating a world where the architects of suffering operate with a dispassionate rationality that foreshadows later cosmic dread. *Le Mulâtre* moves the Gothic hegemony closer to Lovecraftian horror through its articulation of an indifference so profound it mirrors the cosmic void. The "Gods" of this system—the Masters and Legislators—are impervious to suffering; their actions are driven by economic imperative. While Lovecraft's spaces are alien, and Lewis's are contaminated sacred grounds, Séjour's plantation functions as an "Economic Laboratory." Its horror emanates from an environment perfectly rational and efficient in its cruelty, asserting that the individual is insignificant within the machinery of the world.

The "Ecstasy of Decay" in Lewis's work depicted the body as a site of "Sin"; Séjour redefines it as a site of "Appraisal" and commodity. The physical trauma inflicted upon Zélie and Georges is a consequence of their status as objects. This "Objectification of the Flesh" establishes a precursor to Body Horror, emphasizing the physical manifestation of systemic violence. Séjour crafts a world where the "Rational Order" of the Law is a deceptive mask for Primal Chaos. To the enslaved, the Law makes no discernible sense; it is a capricious, hungry entity, a terrifying "Horror of Wrong Math" that resonates with the disorienting logic of modern cosmic dread. This examination of systemic structures aligns this section with Pillar A: The Invasive Breach.

Victor Séjour executed the necessary "Secularization of the Damned," relocating the source of horror from the monastery to the marketplace. He demonstrated that the Unbroken Chain of Dread was being forged anew in the iron of American slavery—an institution codified by law and ratified by commerce. By seizing the institutional corruption explored by Lewis, Séjour established it as a potent American innovation in terror. His structural legacy is the creation of the Systemic Gothic, a framework that reveals the most terrifying monster to be one with an unimpeachable legal right to exist. This architect provided the horrifying bridge for the next evolutionary step. Once the human body was codified as "property," the stage was set for a deeper audit of the Fragmented Identity. The subsequent architect must confront the psychological consequences of this status, moving the core of dread from the Legislative Trap to the Horror of the Stolen Self. The terrain was now prepared for William Wells Brown, thus deepening the exploration of Pillar A and beginning the turn toward Pillar C: The Experimental Psyche.

Chapter 13: William Wells Brown: The Architecture of the Stolen Self: The Cadastral Labyrinth of the Self

Victor Séjour's identification of the Systemic Trap performed the necessary secularization of the Gothic, shifting the source of damnation from the monastery to the legislative assembly; this foundational work established the external machinery of legal horror, proving that institutions, not specters, were the true architects of terror. However, while Séjour focused on the explicit, visible mechanisms of the Law, a profound structural void remained regarding the intricate, agonizing internal experience of the "Property-Body," a lacuna awaiting an architect of psychological terror. This void was definitively filled by William Wells Brown (1814–1884), whose seminal work, *Clotel; or, The President's Daughter* (1853), alongside his harrowing fugitive narratives, codified the precise Gothic of Displacement. Brown's oeuvre proved that the American System imprisoned the physical body and irrevocably fragmented the soul, forcing the protagonist into a terrifying, performative existence in which personhood itself functioned as a mask, subject to instant redaction by the State's will. This existential precarity formed the very bedrock of a new architectural horror, one built not of stone, but of shattered identity, a testament to the system's profound capacity for spiritual annihilation.

Thematic Anchor: The Fragmented Persona

The philosophical premise of self-sovereignty holds that an individual's identity emanates from an inalienable core, a truth that Brown's narratives expose as a cruel deception; his work draws on the Gothic trope of the "Tragic Reveal" to reveal the fundamental instability of American identity. The Subversion of Lineage serves as a horrifying genetic axiom: the narrative follows the daughters of Thomas Jefferson, born into the abject condition of slavery. This creates a "Haunted Pedigree," a perversion where the highest symbol of American Liberty is simultaneously the direct architect of the protagonist's profound enslavement. The horror is the biological proof of a father who is also an absolute Master, a structural atrocity embedding moral rot at the nation's core (Pillar B), forcing an internal schism that denies all filial sanctity.

The very essence of selfhood becomes a theatrical deception in Brown's narratives, a continuous act of self-erasure; the narrative is defined by "Passing," a perilous performance functioning as a survival mechanism in which the protagonist must mimic whiteness. This perpetual masquerade demands constant, debilitating vigilance, eroding the authentic self through relentless suppression. The dread stems from the omnipresent threat of the Structural Reveal: if the "mask" slips, the protagonist is instantly reverted from a Person to a mere

Asset. This systemic erasure constitutes a profound psychological violence, manifesting the horror of identity as a contingent construct. The physical expanse of the continent offers no solace; Brown's protagonists are relentlessly pursued across a landscape imbued with menace. Brown architected a Moving Cage as his Gothic, a portable prison where the walls are invisible but omnipresent. Even in nominally "Free" territory, the malevolent shadow of the Fugitive Slave Act functions as an invisible, spectral chain, binding the individual to their commodified past (Pillar A), ensuring an inescapable, pervasive dread that saturates every physical space.

Thematic Anchor: The Fugitive Architect

The lived experience of William Wells Brown constitutes a direct, biographical blueprint for his architectural horrors; his life was a literal enactment of the "Gothic Escape." The Fugitive Architect, born into enslavement and later escaping to the North and Europe, traversed the agonizing transition from "Property" to "Person." This passage marked a profound ontological shift, fraught with peril, and embedded within his psyche was the "Anxiety of Re-Capture." This anxiety represents the psychological reality that once a human body has been codified as property by the Law, its claim to autonomous personhood remains perpetually tenuous, never truly "un-written" from the grand ledger of the State. This indelible mark functions as a constant, internal shadow, a ghost of past ownership.

Brown's multifaceted engagement with letters solidified his position as a Multi-Hyphenate Witness; as a novelist, playwright, and historian, he employed every available literary tool to perform a comprehensive audit of the American System. He recognized that the "Black Experience" was inherently Gothic because it involved inhabiting a world defined by secret histories, the violent theft of names, and the silent horror of hidden graves. This perspective allowed him to anatomize the systemic machinations that transformed individual lives into narratives of terror. His transatlantic journey positioned Brown as an International Auditor, granting him critical distance. He perceived the United States not as a fledgling democracy but as a "Haunted House," a grand structure built upon moral compromise and historical atrocity, which the rest of the world observed with a mixture of horrified fascination and profound dread.

Thematic Anchor: The Stolen Name and the Auction Altar

The very fabric of domesticity, traditionally a bastion of safety, is re-engineered by Brown into a site of profound violation; his architecture of dread relies fundamentally on the subversion of these intimate spaces. Poe localized guilt within the home; Brown proved that the American Home was a structure built upon a foundation of fundamental Moral Rot (Pillar B). The domestic space becomes a site of insidious surveillance where the "Family" unit frequently functions as a predatory organization, complicit in the commodification of human beings. This corruption of the familial bond represents a core horror. The act of naming, a fundamental declaration of selfhood, becomes a casualty of the system; a recurring dread in Brown's work is the Stolen Name, representing a deliberate erasure of identity.

When a person is sold, their given name—and thus their entire history and lineage—is systematically erased, supplanted by a new designation dictated by ownership. Brown demonstrates this as a psychological erasure, a stripping away of the very narrative of existence, rendering the individual a blank slate. The economic infrastructure of the system is the ultimate stage for dehumanization; Brown literalizes the "Anatomy of Terror" by depicting the auction block as the site where the human body is fragmented into a mere list of physical attributes and market prices. This public dissection of personhood represents the secular equivalent of Lewis's "Judgment," but here, the judge is a clerk armed with a ledger. The horror is tangible: bureaucratic commodification—a chilling display of objectification in which the value of a human being is reduced to a series of bids (Pillar A)—the auction block functions as an altar where personhood is immolated for profit.

Thematic Anchor: The Anatomy of Terror: Cognitive Dissonance

The very ground of objective reality becomes unstable for Brown's protagonists; his anatomy of terror relies profoundly on the concept of "Unreliable Reality." The protagonist lives in a state of debilitating Cognitive Dissonance, a psychic fracture. They are explicitly told they are "sub-human" while simultaneously expected to perform complex labor and navigate social roles that require acute intelligence. This inherent, systemic contradiction—the fragmentation of perceived reality versus demanded function—is a direct precursor to the exploration of "Psychological Collapse," demonstrating how external systemic pressures can induce internal mental dissolution (Pillar C).

The public sphere becomes a stage for coerced performance; in *The Escape, or, A Leap for Freedom*, Brown utilizes the theatrical stage to dramatize how Black characters must meticulously "act" to secure survival. The terror is the active Erasure of the True Self beneath the relentless performance of the "Contented Slave." This constant dissimulation hollows out the individual, creating a spectral presence, a social ghost existing only as a reflection of white expectation. The self becomes a performance, a tragic spectacle of enforced non-existence. The ancient Gothic motif of flight is rendered literal; the "Monster" in the woods is not a spectral revenant but a "Slave Catcher"—a corporeal extension of the Law, armed with explicit legal authority. This re-definition transforms abstract dread into a concrete, imminent physical threat. The wilderness becomes an extension of the prison system, a labyrinth where every rustle of leaves portends capture.

Thematic Anchor: The Lovecraft Metric

Brown stands as a necessary bridge because he unequivocally proves that the "System" itself functions as an indifferent, cosmic force; it possesses immense, crushing power that operates without regard for individual human suffering. Environmental Horror manifests as a Cursed Geography: the American South is a Cursed Space, its soil contaminated by generations of unburied history. Brown's land is "Alienated" by human greed, making it fundamentally hostile. The geography functions as an indelible witness, echoing the silent screams of the oppressed. Its vastness offers no escape, only endless repetition of its embedded evils.

The Ecstasy of Decay finds a parallel in Brown's conception of the Asset-Body: the human body is transformed into a Corporeal Cage, its very substance imbued with "Market

Value." Lovecraft sought a liberation from the limitations of the flesh; Brown's characters seek liberation from the Legal Ownership of their flesh. Both architects identify the body as a site of profound restriction, but Brown roots this in the tangible calculus of ownership. Brown's Logic of the Paradox mirrors Conceptual Chaos: the chaos is the Legal Paradox of a democracy that systematizes chattel slavery. This "Wrong Math" of the soul creates a world that is inherently and irredeemably irrational. Brown's work exposes a cosmic absurdity not in alien entities but in human-made laws. Finally, the Fantasy of Order becomes Brown's Fatalism: even when freedom is achieved, the scarring trauma of enslavement remains an unyielding specter. This non-redemptive view of history constitutes a key structural step toward the nihilism of the 20th century.

William Wells Brown successfully evolved the "Systemic Trap" into the profound "Horror of Fragmented Identity." By focusing on the psychological toll exacted by property status and the necessity of "Performance" for survival, he proved that the American Gothic served as a laboratory for the systematic destruction of the Self. His architectural innovation lies in the internalization of the external chains, transferring the locus of horror from the visible dungeon to the invisible confines of the mind. The structural legacy of Brown is the definitive creation of the Psychological Perimeter, an omnipresent boundary within the mind that dictates existence. He proved that the "Monster" was fundamentally the terrifying Void of Identity created by the system itself. This provided the essential bridge for the next architect. Once the Self was anatomized as a "Fragmented Performance," the stage was set for the biological breach. Having explored the horror of the Stolen Self (Brown), the hegemony would now explore the horror of the Stolen Life, not merely as a legal status but as a material composition. The next architect must take this "Commodified Body" and subject it to the ultimate scientific transgression: forcing life into what society has rendered inert. The time was now ripe for Mary Shelley.

Chapter 14: Mary Shelley: The House of Scientific Abomination

The structural evolution of the Gothic reached a pivotal threshold with the consecutive innovations of Victor Séjour and William Wells Brown. Séjour had successfully stripped the genre of its medieval supernaturalism, grounding the "Dread of the Other" in the cold, secular reality of the Systemic Trap. At the same time, Brown deepened this audit by documenting the Fragmented Identity of the commodified self. Together, they proved that a human could be rendered a "Monster" through the mere stroke of a legislative pen. This identification of the Socially Constructed Abomination provided the perfect architectural foundation for the genre's ultimate biological transformation. The next structural architect, Mary Shelley (1797–1851), took the "Property-Body" of the systemic era—a body previously defined and psychologically fractured by legal frameworks—and subjected it to the "Scientific Breach." Her novel Frankenstein; or, The Modern Prometheus (1818) replaced the legal ghost and the systemic victim with the Scientific Monster, cementing the modern dread that the source of fear lies not in ancient curses but in human hubris and the fundamental transgression of natural law through technology. This shift marks a profound move from the Systemic Malice of the American pioneers to the Experimental Psyche of the industrial age, where the "Discarded Matter" of society is reanimated only to be abandoned by its creator.

Thematic Anchor: The Scientific Monster

True terror resides in the dissolution of established boundaries, especially those governing life itself; Shelley's work definitively maps this horrifying dissolution. Shelley's novel is the stark chronicle of Victor Frankenstein, a young Swiss scientist driven by an "unbridled thirst for knowledge" to access the very secret of life. His ambition, a corrosive force, is entirely divorced from moral education; it operates without ethical constraint, embodying a pure form of Pillar B: The Symmetrical Debt (Moral Rot). Victor employs modern science—specifically, Galvanism, a nascent technology of reanimation—to animate a creature assembled from "stolen body parts." This literal "stitching together" of the dead, a grotesque act of biological carpentry, creates a material abomination that definitively replaces the spiritual demons and folkloric specters of the past, marking it as a terrifying product of Pillar C: The Experimental Psyche.

Repelled by his own creation's physical form, Victor flees the immediate scene of his transgression. This act of abandonment mirrors the "Systemic Neglect" found in the American Gothic. Yet it possesses a more personal, visceral cruelty, establishing the creator's ethical failure as the true, internal source of the horror, a direct emanation of Pillar B. The creature, isolated and rejected by a society incapable of seeing past its horrific exterior, seeks a bloody reckoning, not merely out of malice, but from a profound anguish rooted in its creator's dereliction. The quest for life dissolves into a cycle of brutal revenge, claiming the lives of Victor's loved ones and proving that a creation born of moral neglect is a permanent, inescapable moral debt. The chase culminates in the frozen, desolate Arctic. Victor dies, consumed by his pursuit, and the monster vows to immolate himself. The horror is absolute and secular; there is no heaven or hell to adjudicate the crime, only the cold, indifferent ice of the North witnessing humanity's self-inflicted ruin, a bleak, unredeemed landscape of utter desolation.

Thematic Anchor: The Haunted Summer and Galvanic Genesis

The genesis of monumental terror frequently correlates precisely with periods of profound personal and societal disruption; Mary Shelley's "Source Code" was forged in these fires of Romanticism and the cold, absolute reality of personal loss. Conceived during a ghost story contest in Switzerland, amid "the year without a summer"—a period of global atmospheric gloom following a volcanic eruption—the novel was born amid literal and metaphorical darkness. This environmental anomaly provided a pervasive sense of the uncanny that perfectly mirrored the intellectual tumult of its creation. Discussions on Galvanism, the revolutionary scientific concept of using electricity to stimulate dead tissue, allowed Shelley to ground her fantastic premise in contemporary scientific possibility, moving away from Séjour's legalistic frameworks toward a raw, biological reality.

This fascination with the mechanical reanimation of organic matter became the absolute cornerstone of her narrative's scientific plausibility and ethical challenge, directly embodying Pillar C. Furthermore, the profound loss of her prematurely born child in 1815 directly informed Victor's "perverse, unnatural creation," solidifying the novel's core themes of the precarious nature of biological life and the profound responsibility inherent in creation. This intensely personal sorrow endowed the narrative with an undeniable emotional veracity, making the horror of the abandoned creation a deeply felt, rather than merely intellectual, dread, linking the Experimental Psyche to the Symmetrical Debt of moral consequence.

Thematic Anchor: The Perversion of the Natural Order

Human societal structures are eternally vulnerable to collapse when ambition outstrips the foundational tenets of ethical conduct; Shelley's architecture of dread centers on this very anxiety: that the pursuit of knowledge had outpaced moral restraint. Victor's creation is not merely a transgression; it is a direct, blasphemous usurpation of the natural hierarchy, an act of Promethean arrogance. By seizing the power of creation, he triggers a systemic collapse of his own reality, unraveling his family, his sanity, and his future. Shelley established the core tenet of bio-horror with absolute clarity: that science without responsibility leads inevitably to the "Unintended Monster." The absence of an ethical framework is not merely a flaw; it is the ultimate precondition for the emergence of atrocity, a chasm of Pillar B that swallows all reason.

The creature is fundamentally a "Property of Science," a physical object constructed from the discarded, reanimated matter of the graveyard. Its existence is a testament to the absolute horror of synthetic life, a monstrous collage of desecrated parts, each stitch a violation of organic integrity, signifying a profound reduction of life to mere components, a stark embodiment of Pillar C. The novel explores the profound sociological horror of the rejected body—a body so inherently repulsive that society universally refuses to grant it personhood or empathy. This unyielding societal judgment, much like the dehumanizing mechanisms applied to the "Legal Ghosts" of Séjour's South, condemns the creature to an existence of perpetual alienation and suffering. This brutal external judgment reflects deep-seated moral failures (Pillar A and Pillar B).

Thematic Anchor: The Lovecraft Metric

The human capacity for dread intensifies in proportion to the receding possibility of divine intervention; Shelley's novel is the necessary secular bridge to Lovecraft, establishing horror as fundamentally material and technological. Shelley's Arctic is not just a cold expanse; it is a precursor to Lovecraft's vast, indifferent cosmos—a sublime environment that offers no comfort and no solace to human imposition. It signals a universe utterly unconcerned with human suffering, an early manifestation of cosmic dread. The creature, assembled from the dead, is the ultimate expression of the Corporeal Cage, a body that signifies only death and decay. Its final immolation is not an act of redemption, but a move toward ultimate annihilation, a primal obliteration that Lovecraft later admired as the ultimate end of all matter.

Shelley establishes that knowledge itself is dangerous, a force capable of unraveling human understanding. This is the fundamental link to Lovecraft's *Necronomicon*, where understanding the truth of the universe leads not to enlightenment, but only to madness and despair, a terrifying manifestation of Pillar C (Experimental Psyche) dissolving into chaos. Shelley offers an unsolvable tragedy, a narrative devoid of external justice or inherent meaning. This absolute nihilism, this stark absence of a benevolent cosmic order, is the first true secular step toward the Lovecraftian worldview, where human efforts are futile against an uncaring, incomprehensible universe. The environmental horror moves from the contaminated sacred ground of Lewis to the indifferent physical laws of nature.

Mary Shelley's *Frankenstein* is the necessary, secular culmination of the Gothic Age. She successfully transitioned the hegemony of horror from the foundations laid by Victor Séjour and William Wells Brown—the Systemic Trap of social and legal oppression—to the Biological Breach, where dread is born of scientific transgression. Her profound themes of the fragmented body and the absolute ethical responsibility of the creator established the foundational tenets for the entire science fiction and bio-horror genres. The structural legacy of Shelley is the creation of the Material Monster, a physical manifestation of human error. By proving that the most terrifying thing a human can encounter is their own creation—a direct consequence of their hubris—she set the stage for the genre's final internal collapse. The time was now ripe for the horror to move from the external laboratory to the labyrinth of the mind. Having explored the horror of the Law (Séjour), the erasure of the Self (Brown), and the hubris of Science (Shelley), the hegemony would now explore the terrifying realization that the "Monster" is not an external assembly, but a fundamental, inherent void within the human spirit. The next architect must take up Shelley's "Scientific Hubris" and internalize it, mapping the architecture of the soul's own disintegration. The stage was now set for Edgar Allan Poe.

The Evolutionary Handoff: From Historical Atrocity to the Pathological Self

The conclusion of Part II marks the final dismantling of the **Secularization of Dread**. Through the architectural developments of Walpole, Radcliffe, and Lewis, we witnessed the transition of horror from the divine pits of the afterlife to the heavy, cursed stones of the ancestral castle. This movement expanded through the vital systemic audits of Séjour and Brown, who proved that the most inescapable "Cursed Space" was not built of brick, but of legislative codes that rendered the human body a commodity. It reached a visceral threshold with Mary Shelley, who took the commodified body and subjected it to the scientific breach, creating a material monster that existed outside the natural order.

The handoff to the next era occurs as the **External Siege**—the law, the plantation, the scientific lab—begins to collapse into the internal psyche. As the Industrial Age accelerated, the Hegemony recognized that the most terrifying labyrinth was not the subterranean vault but the human mind. The "Monster" was no longer an external assembly or a social contract; it was an **Intrinsic Malady** lurking within the individual's biological and psychological architecture.

In the coming chapters, you will witness the **Internalization of the Void**. The site of terror moves from the landscape of the South and the ruins of Europe into the nerves, the blood, and the fractured consciousness. The Unbroken Chain now turns its gaze inward, auditing the soul's capacity for self-destruction and the biological betrayals of the flesh, inaugurating the age of the **Pathological Turn**.

PART III: THE PATHOLOGICAL TURN

The Internalization of the Monster (1850 – 1910)

Chapter 15 Edgar Allan Poe: The Labyrinthine Architecture of the Self: The Psychological Void: A Descent into Self-Generated Terror

The human mind stands as the ultimate architectural construct, a profound and intricate edifice capable of generating its own abyssal horrors. These are not phantoms of external origin but emanations from the very core of consciousness, absolute and self-contained. Following Mary Shelley's precise application of scientific principles to the very fabric of the Gothic body—meticulously detailing the monstrous genesis of Frankenstein's creation and thus establishing a new lineage of visceral dread rooted in scientific hubris—the overarching structural trajectory of the hegemony pivots decisively inward. This reorientation redirects the gaze of terror from the laboratory's monstrous progeny to the mind's internal deformities. The unparalleled architect who definitively perfected the horror of the internal psyche was Edgar Allan Poe (1809–1849), a master who irrevocably shifted the Gothic focus from the vast, external grandeur of the castle—a monumental symbol of inherited societal decay—to the suffocating, labyrinthine architecture of the human mind itself. Poe meticulously established the foundational rules for Modern Psychological Horror, proving that the deepest wellspring of dread emanates from the terrifying certainty of one's own irreversible mental collapse. This fundamental reorientation places his work squarely within Pillar C: The Experimental Psyche, as he dissects the mechanisms of consciousness to reveal its inherent fragility and its absolute power to construct inescapable prisons of madness.

Thematic Anchor: The House as Mind

The internal landscapes Poe constructed are defined by the concentrated "tale of effect," a structural principle that requires every element of a narrative to contribute to a single, unified emotional response: dread. This intellectual rigor forms the spine of his architectural designs. Consider "The Fall of the House of Usher"; here, the physical decay of the mansion functions as an absolute mirror of the mental collapse of Roderick Usher, its final occupant. The fissured facade, the oppressive miasma, and the very sentience attributed to the stones themselves all reflect Roderick's disintegrating intellect.

The horror emerges from the total, terrifying merging of the external environment with an internal, pathological illness, making the edifice a literal extension of the diseased mind—a tangible manifestation of Pillar B's Moral Rot intertwined with Pillar C's psychological disintegration. The narrative itself becomes an immersive descent into a shared pathology, where the reader is inexorably drawn into the Usher family's inherited madness, a curse made manifest in stone and blood. In "The Tell-Tale Heart," the terror is generated entirely by the narrator's self-betrayal, a process of internal corruption that culminates in the auditory hallucination of a beating heart, ceaselessly accusing from beneath the floorboards. The meticulous planning, the warped rationality, and the ultimate, inescapable guilt prove the mind's role as its own relentless inquisitor, a pure testament to Pillar C.

Thematic Anchor: The Imp of the Perverse

Poe's "Source Code" was forged in a life characterized by chronic loss and the specific melancholia endemic to the American South of his era. These biographical pressures created a worldview steeped in a profound sense of doom. This biographical foundation imbues his architectural designs with an unshakeable authenticity of despair; his narratives are not theoretical constructs but visceral experiences of personal torment. As the definitive inventor of the modern detective story, Poe's unique brand of horror is rooted in the hyper-rational mind's valiant yet ultimately futile attempt to manage its own irrational breakdown. This inherent conflict—the futile struggle of reason against an encroaching, internal chaos—becomes a recurring motif, a fault line within the psyche.

Poe also introduced the "Imp of the Perverse"—a primordial, inescapable human impulse toward self-destruction, an innate malevolence that undermines all reason and self-preservation, compelling individuals to act against their own best interests for the sheer sake of transgression. This psychological construct establishes the ultimate internal enemy: the uncontrollable, inherently flawed self, a foundational principle of Pillar C, demonstrating the mind's inherent capacity for moral rot from within. This ideological shift creates a vacuum where self-generated terror flourishes, a potent example of Pillar B's moral decay, where the internal moral authority becomes its own source of profound corruption.

Thematic Anchor: The Architecture of Premature Burial

The cultural architecture of dread within Poe's work relies profoundly on 19th-century anxieties concerning unreliable interiority. Poe took the inherited guilt traditionally associated with the grand, remote castle and meticulously localized it to the intimate, domestic space. The moral decay of the individual homeowner now infects the very walls of the house, rendering the sanctuary a prison. Furthermore, the pervasive dread of premature burial, a profound and widespread fear born of medical ignorance and the precariousness of life in Poe's era, was masterfully deployed.

He utilized the "Body Re-animated"—most notably with Madeline Usher's terrifying return from her tomb—to signify an absolute truth: the past, with its accumulated guilt and unresolved horrors, refuses to stay buried. It will claw its way back to torment the living, a physical manifestation of psychological repression. This element functions as both an external cultural anxiety (Pillar A) and a psychological torment (Pillar C), inextricably linked to ancestral moral rot (Pillar B), proving the interconnectedness of personal, cultural, and moral decay. By forcing the reader into the unreliable narrator's collapsing mind, Poe creates a shared, inescapable claustrophobia. The reader is irrevocably trapped within the narrator's disintegrating intellect, experiencing the horror as an internal, visceral reality.

Thematic Anchor: The Lovecraft Metric

In a comparative analysis, Poe's architectural innovations serve as a crucial precursor to later forms of dread, establishing principles that would be reinterpreted and expanded. He employed the environment as a subjective, metaphorical cursed space, a haunted canvas reflecting internal states and psychological aberrations. H.P. Lovecraft would later take this "atmospheric rot" and transform it into an objective, cosmic force, an impersonal malevolence existing independently of human perception.

Poe's focus on the "Premature Body"—the fear of sentience entombed—contrasts with Lovecraft's later emphasis on external, alien biological decay, highlighting Poe's commitment to human-centric horror. Crucially, Poe's architectural constructions present horror as unsolvable and non-redemptive. There exists no escape, no therapeutic resolution; only an inevitable, inexorable decline into madness or self-destruction. This absolute rejection of resolution represents a key structural step toward the nihilistic architectures that would define Lovecraft's later cosmic dread, a world where humanity is insignificant. Poe cemented the idea that some horrors exist as inherent, unvanquishable truths, fundamental flaws within the human condition itself.

Edgar Allan Poe is the crucial structural bridge that perfected the psychological horror born of the Gothic era. He decisively rejected the sprawling architecture of the Gothic novel, focusing the genre on the concentrated dread of the internal landscape. By rendering the protagonist as both the unreliable narrator and the architect of his own destruction, Poe cemented the theme that the most terrifying monster is always the self. This absolute internalization of terror defines his legacy. The hegemony now demands a re-externalization of this internal rot. Having meticulously mapped the "Void of the Mind," the Unbroken Chain must now return to the "Void of the Land." The next architect must take Poe's "House of Usher"—that potent symbol of decaying, ancestral guilt and personal dissolution—and transplant it back into the foundational soil of the American South, revealing that the madness of the individual is fundamentally inseparable from the madness of a haunted social order. The stage was irrevocably set for the transition from the Psychological Void to the Conjured System. It was time for Charles W. Chesnutt.

Chapter 16 Charles W. Chesnutt: The Plantation as Malign Organism: An Anatomy of Systemic Enthrallment

The internal, claustrophobic dread established by Edgar Allan Poe proved that the true monster was the collapsing self; a revelation, however, confined to the individual's psychic landscape. Poe's architecture was primarily subjective—a private labyrinth of the mind. The inexorable structural evolution of the hegemony demanded that this deeply ingrained psychological rot transcend its internal confines and be projected back onto the social landscape, manifesting as an external, palpable horror. The architect who performed this crucial "Systemic Re-externalization" was Charles W. Chesnutt (1858–1932), whose profound "Conjure Stories" (1899) transformed the Southern plantation from a static backdrop into a sentient, predatory architecture of control. Chesnutt bridged Poe's psychological void to the incipient pathological duality of the modern era by proving that in the American South, the "Self" existed as a fragmented entity, trapped within a master-narrative woven from systemic magic and racialized terror. This externalized horror, embodying both Pillar A: The Invasive Breach and Pillar B: The Symmetrical Debt, erected a new, inescapable wing upon the evolving edifice of dread.

Thematic Anchor: The Systemic Conjure

The fundamental philosophical premise of Chesnutt's horror lies in the insidious nature of the Masked Reality, a pervasive deception in which the surface presents order while profound terror festers beneath. His core thematic anchor, the Systemic Conjure, functions as an omnipresent force woven into the very fabric of the plantation's existence. The transgression, vividly illustrated in *The Conjure Woman*, transpires when a Northern white couple attempts to "rationally" acquire a Southern plantation, approaching the transaction with a naive faith in simple commerce. This act represents a profound intellectual hubris; the transgression is the belief that land, steeped in generations of exploitation, can be owned through economic exchange while ignoring the spiritual blood-debt embedded in the soil.

The transformation, a recurring horror in "The Goophered Grapevine" and "Po' Sandy," involves humans being transmuted into inanimate objects or plants; this is a literal, biological reduction designed to facilitate forced labor. This phenomenon is the ultimate Objectification of the Flesh, where the "Property-Body" becomes a literal, organic extension of the landscape. A spectral entity does not initiate the pursuit and collapse, but by the "Goopher"—the omnipresent Curse itself. The plantation functions as an inescapable "Closed Loop," where the established laws of nature are suspended and rewritten by the capricious laws of the Master. The resolution offers no catharsis; the Northern “Rationalist” remains willfully oblivious, while the reader is left with the terrifying realization that the plantation’s history is a permanent, active haunting.

Thematic Anchor: The Architect of the Color Line

Chesnutt’s architectural genius was forged within the crucible of the “Post-Reconstruction” era, a period defined by the systematic legal “unmaking” of Black personhood. His lived experience provided the “Source Code” for his incisive audit; born with a “fair” complexion, he possessed the capacity to “pass” for white, yet he resolutely chose to identify as Black. This profound duality granted him an unparalleled vantage point, allowing him to understand that identity in America was a Legal Fiction and a crushing Psychological Burden. As Poe’s successor, Chesnutt addressed a specific gap: Poe identified the internal abyss; Chesnutt explained the Environmental Cause and the structural means by which this abyss was maintained.

The moral decay and collapse of the House of Usher was thus reframed as the pervasive, systemic rot of the House of Slavery. The Architecture of the “Double-Talk” became his primary narrative tool; Chesnutt utilized the “Frame Narrative” to mimic the inherent duality of the Southern Black experience. Uncle Julius’s tales, ostensibly offered as quaint folk stories, function as a psychological “Mask”—a sophisticated structural architecture designed to protect the storyteller's vulnerable self while launching a potent, veiled critique against the oblivious master class. This intricate narrative layering became the foundational blueprint for a horror that spoke truth through strategic concealment.

Thematic Anchor: The Rationalist's Blindness

Chesnutt's architecture of dread is founded upon Identity Instability and the failure of Northern Rationalism to comprehend the true nature of Southern horror. The Horror of Systemic Hypocrisy forms the bedrock of this dread; the stories relentlessly assault the myth of the "Benevolent Plantation," revealing it as a vast site of Moral Rot (Pillar B). The "Master" is the primary source of the supernatural malignancy; his will has been transmuted into a malevolent energy that saturates the land. The Rationalist's Blindness is embodied by the Northern narrator, John, whose attempts to apply "Economic Logic" prove utterly futile.

His inability to perceive the visceral horror embedded within Julius's tales demonstrates that the "Rational Mind" is structurally incapable of confronting a Systemic Curse that operates beyond its empirical framework. Conversely, the Conjure as Resistance provides the only authentic counter-architecture. The "Conjure Woman," Aun' Peggy, possesses a magic that functions as a "Secular Demon," a force the dominant system cannot control. This potent, primal magic establishes a terrifying "Shadow Law" operating beneath the white legal code, a reminder that not all power flows from the visible structures of authority, and that a deep, primordial external force (Pillar A) actively contests the hegemony.

Thematic Anchor: Biological Transmutation: The Body as Timber

Chesnutt's precise anatomy of terror rests upon Biological Transmutation and the "Sentient Environment." The Mechanics of the Transmutation, particularly the transformation of a man into a tree in "Po' Sandy," represents a key mechanical difference in Chesnutt's horror. This is not a symbolic act; it is a literal, irreversible alteration of biological state, a process that strips away personhood. From Property to Matter, this transformation anchors the horror in the physical world. The ultimate horror is the absolute Loss of Biological Autonomy. Sandy is not "haunted" by a spirit; he *is* the spirit, irrevocably trapped within the inert wood of the master's house—a grotesque architectural integration.

Chesnutt skillfully employs the Southern landscape as a literal mirror reflecting the diseased social state. The "Goophered" grapevine literalizes a contaminated economy, a manifestation of the toxic value placed on human life. The soil itself becomes "cursed" by the blood of the enslaved laborers, a biological debt that permeates the foundation of the plantation and demands payment. This environment does not merely witness atrocity; it becomes an active, malevolent participant. This environment-as-organism ensures that the horror is inescapable, as the very resource of life (the land) is turned into a mechanism of imprisonment.

Thematic Anchor: The Lovecraft Metric

Chesnutt provides the necessary bridge from the "Individual Madman" of Poe to the "Systemic Monster" that would later haunt Lovecraft's cosmos. His contribution to Environmental Horror is profound; Chesnutt's plantation is an "Ordered Labyrinth," a seemingly rational system where monstrosity thrives as an intrinsic component. This lays the conceptual groundwork for Lovecraft's "Decaying Rural" aesthetic. The Ecstasy of Decay finds its precursor in Chesnutt's Commodified Body. Here, the horror is the absolute Malleability of the Flesh; humans are transmuted into lumber or grapes for economic expediency.

This stark view of the body as "Raw Material" for a higher, indifferent power—be it The Master or The Conjure—establishes a direct conceptual link to Lovecraft's cosmic indifference. Conceptual Chaos is fundamental; Chesnutt's Fatalism reveals that the ultimate horror is Systemic Determinism. The individual cannot escape the "Goopher" of the State. The chaos resides in the realization that the "Law of the Land" is not a logical construct, but an insidious form of Dark Magic, a perversion of natural order that traps and consumes all within its bounds. The individual's physical form is a fungible asset, a premonition of the biological horror to follow.

Charles W. Chesnutt completed the critical re-externalization of the Gothic framework. He definitively replaced the "Internal Impulse" of individual psychological collapse with the "Systemic Conjure," creating a comprehensive horror template where the enemy is the very fabric of the social and legal order. This evolution established that horror could emanate from the collective, entrenched will of a corrupt society. The hegemony, having externalized this terror, now required a final, chilling internalization of this systemic dread. The "Social Mask" now had to become the "Chemical Mask," a literal transformation from within. The next architect must take this systemic anxiety over "Duality" and the brutal concept of "Property" and fuse them into a pathological reality, where the hidden monster is released from within the "Respectable Gentleman" through a scientific draught. The stage was set for the Pathological Self, and who better to deliver it than Robert Louis Stevenson?

Chapter 17: Robert Louis Stevenson: The Chymical Annex of Internal Dissolution

The systemic re-externalization performed by Charles W. Chesnutt established the Southern landscape as a sentient architecture. This "Goophered" reality trapped the individual within its inescapable psychic and physical confines. This monumental revelation of externalized dread necessitated a subsequent clinical internalization of this duality. The architect who successfully bridged Chesnutt's systemic mask—a social and defensive construct—to the individual biological body was Robert Louis Stevenson (1850–1894). In *The Strange Case of Dr. Jekyll and Mr. Hyde* (1886), Stevenson transformed the concept of a "Conjured Identity" into a pathological, chemical reality. He seized the "Property-Body" of the past. He revealed it to be a new site of internal biological insurrection, establishing the modern dread of the inherent failure of the rational self. Stevenson's work inaugurated a new wing of terror, the Chymical Annex, devoted to the dismemberment of the psyche, placing it squarely within Pillar C: The Experimental Psyche.

Thematic Anchor: The Scientific Double

The fundamental premise of human existence, as posited by Stevenson, is a duality; an inherent schism divides every individual. Stevenson's core thematic anchor is the horror of the Chemical Self, a monstrous entity born from scientific hubris, and the catastrophic failure of Victorian society's rigid repression. Dr. Henry Jekyll, a respected physician and a paragon of Victorian propriety, is consumed by an obsession to surgically separate the "good" and "evil" elements of his nature. He rejects the precedent of the "external conjure"; instead, Jekyll employs the material methodologies of chemistry to formulate a transforming potion. This potion represents a scientific transgression against the natural order of the integrated self.

The creation is Edward Hyde, a being of pure evil liberated from moral constraints. Hyde manifests as small, deformed, and inspires "uncontrollable disgust" in all who encounter him; he embodies the primitive "source code" of the human psyche. The horror intensifies through the legalistic investigation conducted by Mr. Utterson, a rationalist figure attempting to impose order on a chaotic reality. Utterson's failure to comprehend Jekyll's decay mirrors the Northern narrator's previous failure in Chesnutt's work; reason buckles before the truth. The true horror resides in the revelation that the respectable self and the monstrous self are the same. The monster is not an external assembly, as Frankenstein's creation was to Shelley, but a fundamental, scientific, and internal part of the self—a biological inevitability.

Thematic Anchor: The Architecture of Repression

The late nineteenth century was an era defined by accelerating medical advancement and deep public anxiety over Degeneration Theory, which posited a biological regression of humanity. Stevenson grounded the transformation of Jekyll into Hyde in explicit chemical causation, reflecting the period's advances in pathology. The monster is a pathological reality, a testament to scientific discovery revealing inherent human corruption. Stevenson's work addressed the "mask" left by Chesnutt. While Chesnutt's masks were social stratagems, Stevenson's mask—the respectable facade of Jekyll—is a chemical failure, a thin barrier dissolved by internal biological forces.

This shift led to the construction of a Chymical Annex, a specialized laboratory within the House of Horror, where the focus shifted from societal machinery to cellular mutation. The architecture of repression found its ultimate metaphor in Jekyll's struggle; his attempts at rigid self-control proved futile against the biological consequences of his own base desires. The novel stands as an enduring testament to the futility of the "Respectable Gentleman" to escape the inherent, chemically inscribed flaws of his own physical being. This moral decay (Pillar B: The Symmetrical Debt) is not a supernatural curse but a pathological consequence of the experimental psyche (Pillar C).

Thematic Anchor: The Dual Doorway

The edifice of Stevenson's dread is founded on anxieties about Victorian social hypocrisy and the terrifyingly porous boundaries of class identity. The novel assaults the façade of respectability, demonstrating its inherent flimsiness. Hyde's simian quality and his apelike deformity directly tapped into contemporary fears of Darwinian Regression—a chilling counterpoint to the era's belief in evolutionary progress. Stevenson masterfully employed the urban landscape to mirror the internal moral state. The architectural symbolism of Jekyll's house is paramount: the respectable front door, used by Jekyll, represents the public persona.

Conversely, the neglected, sordid back-laboratory door used by Hyde externalizes the home's and Victorian society's internal hypocrisy. This dual architecture of the dwelling physically manifests the divided self, a literal construction of internal moral schism, making the private space a terrifying map of the soul's corruption. The very structure becomes a testament to decay, a physical manifestation of Pillar C. The lawyer, Mr. Utterson, attempts to use legal documents and wills to solve the mystery. His systematic failure proves that the conventional tools of the Victorian establishment are utterly inadequate against this new form of biological rot.

Thematic Anchor: The Lovecraft Metric

Stevenson's work provides the necessary bridge to Lovecraft's scientific fatalism. The cursed space, once the isolated castle, becomes the modern metropolis of London. The horror is that the monstrous self can hide invisibly within the ordered labyrinth of the city. This cursed urban space provides the essential setting for the subsequent urban invasion in Stoker's work. The ecstasy of decay manifests as the biological body's degeneration. Hyde is a symbol of moral and biological regression, a direct link to Lovecraft's later themes of cosmic decay and the inherent fragility of human existence.

The ultimate horror Stevenson reveals is conceptual chaos: the chemical self, Hyde, dominates the rational self, Jekyll, involuntarily, asserting a biological imperative over conscious will. This scientific fatalism, in which the body's internal chemistry dictates destiny, is the necessary stepping stone to Lovecraft's materialist view of a universe in which humanity's agency is an illusion before incomprehensible cosmic forces. The transformation sequence is not a magical event but a chemical reaction, stripping the supernatural of its "moral" choice and replacing it with a "biological" certainty, perfectly aligning with the terminal nihilism of the Lovecraft Metric.

Robert Louis Stevenson fully internalized the Gothic framework. He successfully replaced the Romantic impulse of Poe and the Systemic Mask of Chesnutt with scientific pathology. Stevenson created the modern horror template where the primary enemy is the self, chemically unleashed from its own biological confines. This development constructed the Chymical Annex, a specialized laboratory within the House of Horror, dedicated to the study of the self's internal dissolution. The hegemony now required a re-externalization of this pervasive dread on a global, epidemiological scale. The internal, pathological terror, once confined to a single individual, had to be applied to the larger social body. The next architect was tasked with taking Stevenson's biological anxiety over "degeneration" and fusing it into a massive sociological threat. The doctor's lab's internal monster was destined to become the invading monster threatening the bloodline of the entire British Empire. The stage was undeniably set for the transition from the Pathological Self to the Sociological Vampire. Bram Stoker, you're up.

Chapter 18 Bram Stoker: The Global Contagion Nexus

The late Victorian era, defined by the failure of the rational self, manifested as a profound epistemological crisis, rendering the individual mind permeable to the irrational and the monstrous. Unprecedented urban expansion generated acute anxieties regarding social anonymity and systemic decay. These converging societal tremors necessitated a reorientation of horror's focus; dread must extend its grasp to the largest social unit, the city itself. The architect who decisively accomplished this pivotal transition was Bram Stoker (1847–1912). His seminal novel, *Dracula* (1897), meticulously fuses the ancient evil inherent in the Gothic tradition with the emergent scientific fears of contagion and systemic biological threat. Stoker replaced the singular, internal pathological monster with a contaminating foreign predator whose very presence threatens the moral and biological integrity of the British Empire. This systemic, urban dread provides the ultimate Victorian framework, an indelible mark upon the house of horror, before the narrative hegemony returns to the American South to explore the more intimate horror of the Bloodline.

Thematic Anchor: The Vessel of the Past

Stoker's primary thematic anchor establishes the horror of Invasion and the insidious corruption of societal structures. The narrative initiates this cascade of terror with Jonathan

Harker's journey into Transylvania, a geographical locus where modernity's empirical certainties dissolve. He finds himself imprisoned within a castle, a monolithic "Vessel of the Past," a structure actively defying temporal linearity. Its very stones breathe an accumulated, preternatural history that negates scientific progress.

Preternatural powers manifest within these walls, systematically dismantling modern physics and demonstrating the inherent fragility of human-constructed laws. This entrapment represents the enlightened mind held captive by a forgotten history. The Invasion itself then unfolds as a profound act of Reverse Colonialism. Dracula orchestrates his passage into London through "contaminated earth"—a symbolic cargo of ancestral blight that brings him to the heart of the empire. The horror resides in this audacious Reclaiming of the Metropolis by the primitive. Stoker posits that the Empire's expansive ambition invited a parasitic "return of the repressed." This epidemiological threat becomes palpably manifest as Dracula strategically targets the vital blood of Victorian women, transferring his vampiric condition through a Dark Contagion. This process is framed as a biological weapon that threatens to transform respectable citizens into predatory creatures, annihilating the established social order and corroding the foundations of domesticity.

Thematic Anchor: The Technological Occult

A counter-offensive of modern ingenuity emerges within this burgeoning terror. The Scientific Defense, marshaled by Professor Van Helsing, relies upon a precise hybrid of ancient ritual and cutting-edge modern science. They employ blood transfusions as medical intervention, meticulous pathological observation, and the rapid dissemination of intelligence via telegraphs. This unique synthesis constitutes the Technological Occult—the realization that ancient evil demands a sophisticated, modern database for its tracking. Rational inquiry must weaponize the irrational, mapping its archaic power onto contemporary grids of knowledge.

The Resolution culminates in the systematic pursuit and destruction of Dracula by a collective, a testament to coordinated human endeavor. The horror is definitively "solved" through a concerted bureaucratic effort that aims to purify the social body. This suggests a triumph of order, a successful restoration of equilibrium, yet simultaneously foreshadows the vulnerability of such systems to more intractable threats. Stoker's use of the Documentary Form is a crucial architectural element; he employed diaries, ship logs, and newspaper clippings to imbue his narrative with the irrefutable credibility of scientific evidence. By removing a singular, omniscient narrator, Stoker compels the reader to assume the active role of an auditor of a "Cold Case," forcing the intellectual labor of proving the monster's existence through aggregated facts.

Thematic Anchor: The Epidemiology of the Foreign Other

Stoker's cultural architecture of dread is constructed upon anxieties regarding Epidemiology and the threat posed by the Foreign Other. Vampirism as a disease exploits the rising awareness of "Germ Theory," a new paradigm of microscopic, unseen menace. Vampirism is not a spiritual curse; it is explicitly treated as a virulent, blood-borne pathogen. The proposed "Antidote," blood transfusion, itself constitutes a biological crisis involving the intimate exchange of vital fluids.

This concept embodies the ultimate fear: that the national character can be entirely overwritten by the introduction of "Foreign Blood." This biological assimilation represents a total loss of autonomy, rendering the individual an extension of a foreign will. The Violation of Space extends beyond the physical; Dracula invades the sacred biological space of the human body—the blood itself, the very seat of identity. The narrative's climactic return to Transylvania represents a profound act of Purification, an attempt to re-establish the rigid borders of the Empire and momentarily seal off the infectious threat. This act acknowledges the systemic nature of the threat and the need for a total systemic response—a global epidemiology of terror—yet the indelible stain of invasion persists as a permanent scar on the collective psyche.

Thematic Anchor: The Lovecraft Metric

The Anatomy of Terror, particularly the Mechanics of Blood, establishes it as the central currency of power. Stoker replaces the explicit violence of earlier Gothic modes with the insidious Eroticism of the Bite, suggesting a dark, predatory sexuality contaminating the lineage itself. This precise modulation represents the foundational first step toward the Hereditary Gothic, where the corruptions of the past are inscribed biologically. The Collective Defense, a manifestation of Bureaucratic Horror, dictates that the pursuit of Dracula be handled by a team that forms a decentralized administrative network.

The ubiquitous use of modern implements—typewriters, railway timetables, and phonographs—transforms the Gothic chase into a highly organized, Systemic Action. The relentless application of a Logistical Net destroys the vampire. This systemic approach to combating dread also sets a precedent for Environmental Horror. London is treated as a fertile breeding ground for ancient evil, its infrastructure a network for contagion. H.P. Lovecraft would later seize upon this, scaling its scope to encompass a cosmic dimension, replacing the foreign Count with an omnipresent

Extradimensional Entity. Stoker's horror remains Solvable; the collective, armed with empirical data, possesses the strength to annihilate the threat. This restoration, however, merely postpones the inevitable; Lovecraft would eventually shatter this comforting fantasy, proving the collective's utter powerlessness against cosmic, indifferent horrors.

Bram Stoker completed the monumental externalization of horror, transforming the individualized Gothic curse into a Systemic, Epidemiological Threat. By fusing demonic evil with modern anxieties regarding blood and contagion, Stoker provided the definitive blueprint for the "Invading Monster," a creature whose threat demands a collective, administrative response. His contribution marks a critical pivot, extending the house of horror's influence beyond the individual psyche into the collective body politic. The hegemony now demands a refinement of this "Blood-Dread." Stoker's horror focused on the external predator; the subsequent architect must internalize this focus on Heredity and biological Contamination, turning it back toward the American domestic space. The "Foreign Blood" of Dracula must transmute into the "Suppressed Blood" of the American past—an internal, generational burden. The next architect must demonstrate that the most terrifying revelation inscribed within the blood is the hidden, biological memory of a systemic crime. The stage is set for the transition from the

Sociological Vampire to the Ancestral Haunted. Pauline Hopkins had her work cut out for her.

Chapter 19: Pauline Hopkins: The Atavistic Genealogies of American Dread: A Biological Audit

The 19th century witnessed a desperate, albeit fleeting, illusion of order; Bram Stoker's grand narrative presented a solvable, moral world where scientific inquiry could repel the foreign invader. Pauline Hopkins (1859–1930) fundamentally dismantled this precarious comfort, pivoting the terror of the "Blood Horror" from an external threat into an inescapable internal truth. In her seminal 1902 work, *Of One Blood; or, The Hidden Self*, Hopkins profoundly reconfigured Stoker's epidemiological dread into the gnawing Horror of Ancestral Atavism. She taught the genre that the most profound source of dread is not an alien predator encroaching from beyond borders, but the terrifying realization that one's own very blood contains an ancient, suppressed history—a primordial archive of memory that the rational, modern self cannot control. This establishes a new wing upon the edifice of horror: The Biological Lab of Ancestral Memory, a structure dedicated to the internal invasion of self by history, placing her work firmly at the intersection of Pillar B: The Symmetrical Debt and Pillar C: The Experimental Psyche.

Thematic Anchor: The Internal Invasion

Human consciousness often constructs elaborate façades of modernity, believing itself severed from the archaic forces that shaped its genetic inheritance; Hopkins's horror exposes this delusion. Her characters are destroyed by the accidental activation of their own biological history, inscribed in the very marrow of their being. Reuel Briggs, a medical student performing the precarious act of "passing" for white, embodies the ultimate Victorian rationalist. His identity, predicated upon the suppression of inconvenient truths, is catastrophically subverted when he uncovers his own African ancestry. The horror is the Internal Invasion; the dreaded "Other" does not reside across vast oceans, but courses through one's own veins.

This inversion confirms that true terror emanates from the inescapable moral rot (Pillar B) inherent in a society built upon foundational lies. The mind, in its illusory coherence, often conceives of itself as a singular entity; Hopkins, however, utilizes the concept of "Dual Consciousness" to expose the mind's true nature as a series of "hidden chambers" holding secrets beyond recall. Within the forgotten ruins of Telassar, an ancient Ethiopian city, the protagonist unearths tangible evidence of a pre-human civilization. This discovery reveals that "Modern" identity is actually a degraded, amnesiac version of an "Ancient" past—an inferior echo of a grander, more terrible history. This provides the blueprint for cosmic dread, demonstrating that the human psyche is merely a precarious outpost in a vast biological archive.

Thematic Anchor: The Contaminated Map of Pedigree

Pauline Hopkins wrote within the crucible of escalating racial terror and pseudoscientific racism. Her background as an editor and activist equipped her to forge her "Archives of Dread," a literary architecture designed to expose the nation's deepest hypocrisies. She strategically weaponized the Gothic form to demonstrate a chilling axiom: if "Blood" constituted the fundamental currency of American social stratification, then "Blood" was also the site of its ultimate haunting. Victorian society harbored a pathological obsession with racial purity, a delusive pursuit of unblemished lineage. Hopkins recognized this as a constructed fantasy.

Her fiction argued that the American bloodline was not a pristine genealogy, but a vast, Contaminated Map where every family tree was irrevocably rooted in the "Secret Sin" of the plantation. This historical truth served as a festering wound within the collective psyche. Hopkins provided the precise structural handoff to the next generation by shifting the focus from the Pathological Body of individual deviance to the Atavistic Body—a vessel of ancient, collective memory. She developed the concept of the "Ancient Race" surviving as a living, potent presence within the blood of modern individuals. This framework exploits the terror inherent in Hereditary

Memory, in which contact with the "Hidden Self" initiates an irreversible process that collapses the established social identity.

Thematic Anchor: The Failure of Medical Materialism

Western science often asserts its omnipotence in explaining the human condition; Hopkins introduced the chilling terror that this science is profoundly blind. Reuel Briggs's medical training and his rigorous adherence to empirical observation prove incapable of accounting for the "Soul-Phenomena" and ancestral visions he experiences. This demonstrates an absolute failure on the part of medical materialism to grasp the true nature of reality. Hopkins took the urban dread of contagion spreading through the metropolis and localized it to the Domestic Bloodline. The source of evil is the "Secret History" of the American family encoded in genetic material.

The anatomy of terror in Hopkins's oeuvre relies upon the "Medical Record" and the "Visions of the Hidden Self." She masterfully utilizes the fragmented states induced by "Mesmerism" as scientifically plausible pathways to access the deep neurological archives of ancestral memory. This provides the horror with "Scientific Credibility" while proving that the conscious mind is not its own master. The realization of true ancestry is an irreversible transformation—a cataclysmic unmasking. The result is the destruction of the ego and the complete dissolution of any prior sense of self. This spectacle of Biological Truth represents a denial of Western human exceptionalism, demonstrating that the past is an inescapable, living force.

Thematic Anchor: The Lovecraft Metric

Pauline Hopkins stands as the foundational thematic anchor that connects the Systemic Gothic to the nascent Cosmic Gothic. She establishes the terrifying precedent of the "Ancient Entity" residing within humanity's blood—an internal cosmic horror that Lovecraft would later project onto the stars. Environmental horror finds its initial architect here, where space becomes cursed by history. The ruins of Telassar provide the Proto-Cosmic Landscape. The horror resides in its ancient, non-human, and immeasurably vast history that dwarfs human existence. Lovecraft would adopt this "Hidden City" trope wholesale, acknowledging Hopkins's pre-emptive mapping of cosmic dread.

The ecstasy of decay is present in her treatment of the Atavistic Body. The body is a canvas of terror where the skin serves as a mere mask, while the blood reveals the terrifying truth of ancestry. This fear of the "Body as a Traitor"—a biological repository of unspeakable pasts—is a thematic bridge to Lovecraft's later explorations of inherited degeneration. Finally, the fantasy of order is obliterated. Hopkins denies the hope for a "Pure" future, asserting that the marks of the past preclude it. The horror is fundamentally unsolvable because the "Crime"—slavery and miscegenation—is already inscribed in the blood. She provides the biological proof that the collective identity of America is built upon an unaddressed lie.

Pauline Hopkins stands as the indispensable architect of the structural framework who weaponized the Hereditary Gothic, transforming its anxieties into a potent force of cultural critique. She completed the process of transitioning the monster from the "Invading Other" to the "Internal Ancestor." By proving that the most terrifying encounter is the confrontation with the "Archive" of one's own blood, she provided the essential link to the emergent horrors of the 20th century. The hegemony now required an externalization of this biological atavism. The "Hidden Self" in the blood must become the "Hidden Reality" embedded within the earth itself. The "Ancient Race" in the veins must transform into the "Pagan Spirit" lurking in the hills. The stage was set for the transition from the Ancestral Haunted to the Pagan Breakdown. Calling Arthur Machen!

Chapter 20 Arthur Machen: The Surveyor of the Veiled Earth

The internal, biological audit performed by Pauline Hopkins revealed the blood to be a haunted archive of ancestral memory, shattering the Victorian illusion of a "pure" lineage. However, the architectural hegemony of horror required one final, terrifying expansion to move definitively from the Biological Atavism of the individual to the Cosmic Atavism of the world itself. The architect who accomplished this, pushing the genre directly toward Lovecraft's nihilism and firmly establishing Pillar C: The Experimental Psyche as the primary conduit for ultimate terror, was Arthur Machen (1863–1947). Machen's works, including the seminal *The Great God Pan* (1894), introduce the horror of Pagan Atavism and the catastrophic Breakdown of Consensus Reality. He taught that the deepest source of dread resides not in a hidden history within the blood, but in the pervasive existence of a blasphemous, non-human reality just beneath the thin, fabricated veneer of civilization.

Thematic Anchor: The Great God Pan

Humanity constructs its reality upon a fragile scaffolding of assumed order, a comforting illusion of control over a universe inherently indifferent to its existence. Machen's horror dismantles this edifice, exposing the catastrophic consequence of violating the boundary between the known and the ancient forces that predate it. In "The Great God Pan," Dr. Raymond performs a surgical operation designed to open a patient's mind to the "True Reality," a realm of perception beyond human capacity. This experimental breaching of the intellect, a pure manifestation of Pillar C, unleashes Helen Vaughan, who becomes a terrifying agent of cosmic chaos.

The horror of this narrative establishes that the "Source Code" of nature, when glimpsed directly, is too terrible for the human mind to bear, causing immediate dissolution of sanity and form. Machen's narratives refuse the comforting "Solvability" of Stoker; contact with the truth causes not merely death, but a profound moral and biological dissolution. This embodies the Atavistic Survival—the absolute proof that humanity exists as a temporary tenant on an old, alien earth, a fleeting presence in a world governed by elder intelligences. He grounded his horror in the conviction that spiritual realities are operative beneath the superficial skin of modernity, and that certain archives of reality are better left eternally sealed.

Thematic Anchor: The Ancient Reality of the Earth

The intellectual landscape of the *fin-de-siècle*, marked by an exhaustion with positivism, provided the fertile ground for Machen's specific brand of dread. Born in the mist-shrouded landscape of Wales, Machen imbibed the essence of pre-Roman pagan survivals, the hills themselves whispering of elder things.

His immersion in the Hermetic Order of the Golden Dawn laid the foundation for a cosmology in which potent realities are active beneath the surface of the modern world. Machen addressed the problem left by Hopkins: she identified the "Ancient Race" haunting human blood; Machen identified the "Ancient Reality" permeating the earth itself—an external, primordial archive of non-human sentience.

This transition was explicitly praised by H.P. Lovecraft, who lauded Machen for identifying the non-human and indifferent reality. Machen provided the "Pagan Raw Material," the foundational concepts of cosmic nihilism, that Lovecraft would later systematize into the Cthulhu Mythos. Machen exploits Victorian anxiety about atavism but transforms it into an immutable cosmic law. While Hopkins demonstrated regression through Ancestral Memory, Machen depicted it as a pervasive Cosmic Force—an inescapable gravity that pulls humanity back into primordial chaos. The ultimate source of evil is not a hidden family secret, but the landscape itself—the ancient, unreadable earth, a silent repository of blasphemous memory.

Thematic Anchor: The Mechanics of Ontological Annihilation

The human mind resists the comprehension of truths that dismantle its core certainties; thus, the architecture of terror often thrives on implication. Machen perfected the mechanics of suggestion, employing fragmented evidence—disjointed letters and cryptic reports—to construct dread through the deliberate concealment of the full horror. This allows the imagination to fill the voids with unspeakable possibilities. The terror culminates in the visible, grotesque dissolution of the human form upon direct contact with pagan reality.

Helen Vaughan's metamorphosis in "The Great God Pan" provides the ultimate illustration of this physical and spiritual undoing. Her body cycles backward through the chain of being—from woman to beast to a formless mass—a literal un-writing of genetic history. This is the absolute denial of Human Exceptionalism, a chilling testament to humanity's precarious position in a universe that does not recognize its unique form as permanent. Her body becomes a direct conduit for primordial chaos, embodying the ultimate synthesis of dread that humanity is merely a temporary, fragile arrangement of matter, easily dissolved back into the primal flux.

Thematic Anchor: The Lovecraft Metric

Machen's architectural contributions provide the direct blueprint for the cosmic nihilism that defines Lovecraftian horror. His conception of environmental horror, embodied by the ancient Welsh hills, stands as the direct ancestor to

Lovecraft's Arkham. The horror resides within the ancient, indifferent landscape itself, a sentient presence predating human habitation. Machen introduced the explicit horror that consensus reality is a mere illusion, a construct easily shattered by contact with the cosmos' genuine underlying nature.

Lovecraft merely replaced Machen's occult truth with an objective, alien, and scientific one, systematizing the mechanism of cognitive shattering Machen had first established. Machen denies the "Fantasy of Order" that characterized earlier horror; his narratives offer no escape and no possibility of restoring the state of blissful ignorance. He provides the final proof that humanity is irrelevant to the amoral forces of the cosmos, its existence a fleeting anomaly, completing the structural handoff to Lovecraft's full, uncompromising nihilism. He built the definitive wing of cosmic indifference onto the grand architectural design of horror.

Arthur Machen stands as the final structural architect of the pre-cosmic age, the crucial hinge between individual internal terrors and the vast, external, and indifferent cosmos. He completed the process of secularization by introducing the concept of Pagan Dread and the inherent instability of reality as the ultimate sources of terror. By replacing the "Internal Archive" of ancestral memory with the "Primordial Archive" of the earth itself, he provided the essential link to the existential horrors of the 20th century. This structural framework, now fully cosmic in scope, demanded a final author to take these ideas and elevate them to the ultimate, global, and objective philosophical statement. The architectural hegemony now moves to the man who systematized Machen's pagan dread into the modern, fully realized philosophy of Cosmic Indifference. The stage was set for the final transition from the Pagan Breakdown to the Cosmic Apex, and the epitome of the metric we use. The wheels were primed for H.P. Lovecraft.

The Evolutionary Handoff: From the Pathological Self to the Cosmic Void

The conclusion of Part III marks the definitive **Internalization of the Monster**. Through the architectures of Poe, Chesnutt, and Stevenson, the Hegemony proved that the most terrifying labyrinth was the human psyche and the most dangerous predator was the chemical or social "Double" lurking within the self. This era concluded with the sociological and epidemiological expansions of Stoker and Hopkins, who transformed the internal rot of heredity and blood into a global crisis of contagion and atavistic memory.

The handoff to the next era occurs as the **Pathological Turn** reaches its limit. While the architects of the 19th century found horror in the breakdown of the individual, the architects of the 20th century realized that the individual—and indeed the entire human species—is merely a flickering anomaly in an ancient and indifferent universe. The "Monster" was no longer a defect in the blood or a fracture in the mind; it was the **Absolute Truth** of cosmic insignificance.

In the coming chapters, you will witness the **Ascension of the Void**. The site of terror moves from the clinical laboratory and the ancestral home to the cold reaches of space, the non-Euclidean depths of the ocean, and the sentient atmosphere of the land itself. The Unbroken Chain now reaches its maximum scale, auditing the collapse of human meaning in the face of an uncaring infinity, inaugurating the age of the **Hegemonic Apex**.

PART IV: THE HEGEMONIC APEX

Cosmicism and the Modern Synthesis (1910 – 2015)

Chapter 21 H.P. Lovecraft: The Architect of Absolute Incomprehension

The end of the Victorian era posed a definitive challenge to the literary hegemony of horror: the imperative to reconcile a burgeoning scientific understanding of a vast, chaotic universe with the increasingly fragile, outdated comforts of human morality. Howard Phillips Lovecraft (1890–1937) emerged as the architect who delivered the ultimate, devastating answer, constructing a house of terrors that moved decisively beyond the localized pagan dread of Arthur Machen. His philosophical system, Cosmicism, stands as the culmination of the entire Gothic project; it incontrovertibly proves humanity is a "meaningless accident," and its final, terrifying evidence reveals the fundamental disinterest of the universe's laws toward human existence. Lovecraft functions as the prophet of modern, systemic panic, a singular voice articulating the inevitable collapse of anthropocentric delusions. His work is categorized under Pillar C: The Experimental Psyche, for its radical assault upon the very architecture of human consciousness.

Thematic Anchor: Conceptual Chaos

The core thematic anchor of Lovecraft's edifice is the horror of the Unknowable; this truth dictates the inherent futility of human comprehension. The confrontation occurs when the human mind, structured for a finite, terrestrial existence, faces the sheer, incomprehensible scale of the cosmos, losing the geometric and moral structures it needs to perceive any semblance of reality. This intellectual dissolution constitutes a direct assault on the cognitive scaffolding of sapience, dismantling the very means by which humanity constructs meaning. The philosophical premise dictates that the universe operates without regard for human perception or values, a structural reality that collapses all anthropocentric certainty.

The Nihilistic Premise governs Lovecraft's horror, commencing with the inherent inability of the human mind to "correlate all its contents." Understanding the universe invites an unavoidable descent into madness; indeed, the only enduring mercy available to the human condition rests in the perpetuation of ignorance. The mind finds its operating parameters catastrophically exceeded when confronted with truths that defy its innate frameworks. He constructed the Cthulhu Mythos, not as a conventional pantheon of demons, but as "immortal, hyper-scientific entities." These beings represent a reality so ancient and vast that human concepts of "good" and "evil" are utterly irrelevant. The Mythos functions as a structural diagram of cosmic indifference, a diagram whose very existence negates all human exceptionalism, leaving a chilling void where divine judgment once resided.

Thematic Anchor: Non-Euclidean Geometry

Lovecraft's ultimate architectural tool is Non-Euclidean Geometry; this element represents a direct, intellectual assault upon foundational logic. By introducing shapes, angles, and spatial arrangements that cannot exist within three dimensions, he shatters the mind's bedrock certainty, replacing it with a paralyzing, multi-dimensional complexity. This geometrical impossibility functions as a direct corruptor of mental architecture, proving that the very fabric of perceived space is a deceptive construct. This structural evidence of impossible forms induces a visceral dread of sanity's collapse.

Witnessing an "impossible angle" or a geometrically unsound edifice corrupts the mind's very operating system. The integrity of spatial perception, the bedrock of human understanding, is shattered; the mind becomes a defiled temple, its internal logic collapsing under the weight of impossible dimensions. This intellectual assault is a direct and permanent incapacitation. The Final Truth articulated by Lovecraft is the absolute realization of human insignificance; this stands as the zenith of his horror. The Great Old Ones embody "indifferent Disorder"; their existence proves that all human effort is nothing more than a temporary, self-deluding fantasy of order. Humanity's grand structures are but ephemeral etchings upon an infinitely ancient canvas, destined for erasure by forces that do not even acknowledge their presence.

Thematic Anchor: The Anatomy of the Observer

Lovecraft consciously replaced the traditional "Hero" with the "Observer"; this shift is fundamental to his anatomy of terror. The objective is not to defeat a monstrous antagonist, for such an act is inherently impossible against cosmic forces. The goal becomes merely to witness the unimaginable scale of these entities and, if possible, to survive the encounter, albeit with a mind permanently shattered by the experience. The human role is reduced to a passive, terrified sensor, incapable of meaningful action, only able to register the vastness of its own doom.

Lovecraft's biography itself comprises the "proving ground for the horror of the Unknowable." His personal trajectory mirrored the broader cultural anxiety, demonstrating how an individual mind could internalize the impending cosmic collapse. He grounded his horror in the absolute conviction that potent realities are operative beneath the superficial skin of modernity. His environments function as active sources of sensory assault. They manifest through oppressively heavy air and hostile physics. These surroundings are not passive backdrops; they are malevolent extensions of the cosmic horror, actively working to disorient and break the human spirit. The very atmosphere becomes an antagonist, a pervasive, suffocating presence designed to dismantle mental fortitude.

Thematic Anchor: The Lovecraft Metric

Lovecraft's environmental horror fundamentally departs from its predecessors; the physical laws themselves are the source of the curse, rendering escape from the natural order impossible. The landscape is fundamentally wrong, imbued with an alien logic that predicates human suffering. He utterly inverts the Medieval concept of the body, which perceived decay as a judgment for sin; for Lovecraft, decay represents the inevitable return to a formless, cosmic truth. The dissolution of the flesh is a shedding of illusory form, a process that strips away the artificial constructs of humanity to reveal the underlying reality.

Conceptual Chaos constitutes the final, absolute terror within his system. The ultimate revelation is that the human mind's reliance on Euclidean mathematics and predictable physics is a lie. This constitutes the ultimate "Unsolvable," a structural problem that defies all rational inquiry and offers no possibility of resolution, only the certainty of mental collapse. The universe's architecture is a riddle designed to break the interpreter. This intellectual structural evidence synthesizes a pervasive dread of absolute cognitive insolvency. Lovecraft defined the immutable rules of a game where knowledge leads exclusively to madness, and human significance registers as the ultimate "Fantasy of Order."

H.P. Lovecraft stands as the undisputed architect of 21st-century dread. He completed the structural evolution of horror by converting the localized pagan anxiety of Machen into a total, devastating philosophical system. He built a towering black obelisk upon the foundations laid by Machen, a monolithic structure that proved the inherent error of human perception. This constitutes a profound augmentation of the house of horror, adding a colossal wing dedicated entirely to the exploration of the Absolute Void, a chamber of Conceptual Chaos, firmly establishing Pillar C's domain. However, while Lovecraft directed his gaze toward the stars to find an indifferent void, the Hegemony, in its relentless pursuit of terror, required a strategic pivot back to the Terrestrial Void. The "Cosmic Indifference" of the Great Old Ones now needed localization and application to the very soil beneath human feet. The subsequent architect took Lovecraft's established "Environmental Dread" and applied its principles to the American South. This successor proved that the "Indifferent Universe" manifests with palpable menace in the sentient, oppressive atmosphere of the Georgia cane-fields. The stage was irrevocably set for the transition from Cosmicism to the Sentient Environment; the playground of Jean Toomer.

Chapter 22 Jean Toomer: The Aerated Mausoleum of Memory

The Hegemonic Apex established by H.P. Lovecraft confirmed the terrifying philosophical truth that the universe is vast, uncaring, and leads to human insignificance. Lovecraft's dread remained cold and celestial; his horrors inhabited the vacuum of space, detached from the immediate human condition. The structural challenge for the subsequent era mandated the terrestrial embodiment of this "Indifferent Void," applying its chilling principles to the high-heat landscape of the American South. The architect who achieved this transposition was Jean Toomer. In *Cane* (1923), he replaced Lovecraft's "Alien Physics" with an Atmospheric Dread, wherein the land itself—the Georgia dusk, the purple cane—acts as a predatory, sentient force, actively absorbing and erasing the human soul. This marks a critical expansion into Pillar B: The Symmetrical Debt, by demonstrating the corruption inherent in the land's historical burden, and Pillar C: The Experimental Psyche, through its psychological dissolution of identity. It establishes a new wing in the house of horror: the sentient, historically burdened environment.

Thematic Anchor: Atmospheric Erasure

The fundamental truth of existence reveals itself through the land's active participation in human suffering, operating not as a passive stage, but as an inescapable actor in the slow tragedy of being. Toomer's core thematic anchor is the horror of the Sentient Landscape. The Georgia landscape in *Cane* is an active, malevolent entity exerting its will with absolute authority. The "purple haze" and the "smell of boiling cane" are not merely sensory details; they are physical weights that settle over the characters, actively trapping them in a state of terminal longing and racialized trauma. This pervasive atmosphere dictates both consciousness and fate, molding minds as it reclaims bodies.

The land, Toomer posits, exists as "goophered" in a cosmic sense, a universal curse upon the soil. The red dust of Georgia embodies the pulverized history of ancestors; it is a physical manifestation of generational suffering. To walk the land is to inhale the literal essence of systemic crime. The Erasure of the Self forms the terrifying denouement for characters such as Karintha or Fern, who are depicted as being "swallowed" by the horizon. The horror resides in the Loss of Individual Boundaries; the environment asserts such overwhelming power that the discrete human "Self" evaporates into the encompassing atmosphere. The Final Truth is the land's immutable memory of what humanity attempts to forget—an active silence that patiently waits to integrate the living into its enduring, sentient mass.

Thematic Anchor: The Modernist Architect of In-Betweenness

The architect's personal ontology, forged in the crucible of conflicting identities, constitutes the lens through which the fractured reality of the age is rendered. Jean Toomer's biography is a study of identity in-betweenness. Born of mixed heritage and navigating both Black and white social spheres, Toomer rejected the binary "Logic of the Hegemony," a framework he perceived as insufficient for the truth of human experience. He perceived himself as the vanguard of a "new race," an existential positioning that afforded him the clinical, outsider's perspective essential for a true audit of the Southern Gothic's inherent horrors.

As a 1920s Modernist, Toomer employed fragmented poetry and prose as deliberate architectural tools. This fragmentation did not merely reflect a world shattered by the Great War and the Great Migration; it actively replicated that shattering within the reader's experience, dismantling stable reality (Pillar C). The Lovecraftian Pivot in Toomer's work is a critical redirection of cosmic terror. He took Lovecraft's "Environmental Dread" and injected it with a visceral, oppressive heat. Toomer recognized the "Unknowable" manifested terrestrially in the soft, thick dusk of a Georgia evening—an atmosphere capable of concealing a lynching with chilling indifference. This translation of cosmic horror into localized dread signifies a definitive expansion of horror's domain into the intimate and the immediate.

Thematic Anchor: The Failure of the Rational City

The built environment forms a monument to historical inertia, a structural testament that actively suffocates the present. Toomer's architecture of dread finds its foundation in the anxieties of Historical Stagnation and the "Weight of the Air." The narrative's shift to Washington, D.C. introduces The Failure of the Rational City, depicting the metropolis not as a haven of advancement, but as a "Caged Architecture" where the human soul withers, suffocated by artificial constructs and rigid social codes. This urban tableau serves as the definitive blueprint for the Urban Isolation and existential ennui that later architects would perfect.

The Sentient Siege depicts the South as a "Slow Apocalypse," a creeping process of spiritual decay. Toomer's apocalypse is a Permanent Atmosphere—a state where the weight of the past operates as a heavy gas, actively preventing the future from breathing (Pillar B). The Dread of the Cane presents the sugar cane as a recurring "Systemic Monster." It exists as an impenetrable wall of green that conceals unspeakable secrets and absorbs the blood of generations. The cane embodies the Indifferent Continuity of nature, a monstrous, cyclical force that reclaims human suffering into its own unyielding existence. The land, through its persistent physical manifestations, becomes an inescapable, suffocating prison.

Thematic Anchor: The Lovecraft Metric

Architectural evolution dictates that initial frameworks of horror are refined and localized. Toomer stands as the critical "Earthing" architect. He took Lovecraft's vast, astronomical collapse and applied it to the Biological and Social Soil of America, giving it an intimate, inescapable horror. Lovecraft's environmental horror derived from "Alien Physics." Toomer's Environment is ruled by "Historical Physics." The air possesses a palpable heaviness, a direct consequence of past atrocities—a lingering miasma of past violence.

The Ecstasy of Decay for Lovecraft involved "Uncorporeal Liberation." For Toomer, the body is a "vessel of dust" linked to the earth. The horror resides in its absolute Absorption into the Land, where individual matter returns to the soil that embodies generational trauma. Lovecraft's Conceptual Chaos manifested as "Non-Euclidean" geometries; Toomer's Chaos is fundamentally "Non-Linear Time." The past and present coexist in the Southern air, creating a perpetual haunting in which historical trauma is eternally present. The Fantasy of Order remains an illusion. Toomer's Nihilism, akin to Lovecraft's, offers no salvation. The individual exists as a "Meaningless Accident" in the face of the land's vast, cyclical memory.

Jean Toomer provided the essential blueprint for Atmospheric Horror, establishing the landscape as a sentient, predatory force that actively participates in the destruction of the human spirit. He successfully transitioned the hegemony from Lovecraft's "Celestial Indifference" to a terrestrial "Atmospheric Erasure." By making the environment the primary monster, he proved the greatest horror manifested terrestrially, within the very air breathed, making dread unavoidable. The structural legacy of this chapter is the creation of a Cursed Landscape that is "full" of history—a profound architectural modification to the edifice of horror. The structural audit was complete: the "Atmospheric Erasure" of the soil had finally reached its logical endpoint. The narrative hegemony now required a shift from the sentient landscape to the species' ultimate isolation. The "Last Man of the Soil" was destined to become the "Last Man of the World," where the silent, global void of extinction replaces the sentient land. The stage was irrevocably set for the Scientific Siege. The time was now for the transition from the Sentient Environment to the Solitary Survival. The silent winds carried only one name upon them, Richard Matheson.

Chapter 23 Richard Matheson: The Scientific Bastion of Solitude

The existential terror, meticulously constructed by Jean Toomer, confirmed that the very land possessed a malevolent consciousness, capable of dissolving individual identity through the accretion of historical and sensory pressures. This "Sentient Erasure" posed a profound challenge for subsequent architectural endeavors: how to translate such an amorphous, terrestrial dread into the precise, quantifiable lexicon of the mid-20th-century Atomic Age. Richard Matheson (1926–2013) materialized this transformation, crafting a bridge from the primal void of the earth to the sophisticated, often invisible, mechanics of modern epidemiological horror. His seminal work, *I Am Legend* (1954), stands as the definitive blueprint for the Modern Apocalypse, rendering the cessation of civilization a phenomenon of scientific rigor, grounded in verifiable pathology; a deeply personal affliction, experienced within the besieged sanctuary of the individual body; and a profound, unyielding solitude, a condition that strips away all social artifice. This narrative thereby grounds cosmic annihilation in the immediate, tangible reality of individual experience. Matheson's work fits squarely within Pillar A, addressing external, systemic threats through a scientific lens, yet simultaneously exploring the Experimental Psyche of isolation, placing it firmly within Pillar C, where the boundaries of the self are tested and redefined by extreme conditions.

Thematic Anchor: The Scientific Siege

The architecture of *I Am Legend* constructs a thematic anchor around the horror of Isolation and the individual's relentless struggle against a systemic, biological monster. Robert Neville, the last surviving human, inhabits a world stripped of companionship, his existence defined by a meticulous, monotonous routine. These "rituals of order" comprise a desperate and necessary attempt to impose meaning upon an anomic reality, echoing the futile yet defiant endeavors of earlier architects who sought to contain chaotic forces through structure and repetition; these daily acts are a deliberate construction of sanity against utter solitude. Neville's life becomes a series of empirical investigations, each observation a desperate grasp for control in a universe that has rendered human supremacy obsolete. The scientific war he wages unfolds not through the superstitious rites and mystical artifacts employed by Stoker's characters, but through the rigorous application of Medical Materialism, a cold epistemology.

Neville's laboratory becomes a sanctuary of objective truth, where the pathogen's pathology, a specific bacillus, is meticulously researched, its properties cataloged, its weaknesses probed. This redefines horror as a public health crisis, stripping it of spiritual or supernatural pretense and imbuing it with cold, biological inevitability, a rational conclusion to humanity's dominion. The true terror resides in the clinical diagnosis of humanity's extinction, a testament to nature's indifferent, systemic power, a stark manifestation of Pillar A's external threat. The narrative culminates in a final, devastating revelation: Neville encounters an evolved social order of the infected. This new society, born from the ruins of the old, perceives him as the monster, the dangerous anomaly, the grotesque relic of an extinct world, a profound reordering of perceived reality. This horror of inversion exposes a fundamental truth: Neville realizes his role as the "vampire" of this new civilization, a figure of archaic dread. The apocalypse's end is not salvation; it is the terrifying realization that Normality is a Statistical Fact, a designation determined by the numerical preponderance of a species, reducing human exceptionalism to a bygone demographic statistic, thereby dissolving the foundations of his identity.

Thematic Anchor: The Cold War Epidemic

Richard Matheson's literary edifice emerged from the crucible of the 1950s, an era indelibly marked by the pervasive anxieties of the Cold War and the existential threat of the Atomic Age. This cultural backdrop, laden with fears of invisible enemies and societal conformity, permeates every brick of his constructed dread, manifesting as the Epidemiological Shift in horror's landscape. Matheson meticulously replaced the "vague, heavy atmosphere" cultivated by Toomer with the immediate, visceral horror of Viral Contagion, a threat both internal and external. His apocalypse is grounded in the chilling possibilities of biological warfare and mutation, directly reflecting 1950s fears of invisible, uncontrollable forces such as radiation, insidious pathogens, and the silent peril of ideological conformity. The enemy is microscopic, pervasive, and democratic in its devastation, stripping humanity of its collective defense, a clear expression of Pillar A.

As a prodigious screenwriter for *The Twilight Zone*, Matheson honed his craft as a Television Architect, mastering the techniques of "Quiet Terror" and the devastating Twist Ending. These narrative devices served as instruments; they systematically dismantled the reader's moral certainty, forcing a re-evaluation of assumptions about good, evil, and the nature of reality itself, creating structural disorientation within the viewer's psyche. The psychological impact of these inversions echoed the uncertainty of an era perpetually on the brink, engaging Pillar C's experimental psyche through sudden shifts in perspective. This period marks a crucial Toomer-Lovecraft Handoff: Matheson expertly distilled Lovecraft's grand, cosmic scale of annihilation and Toomer's pervasive environmental erasure, bringing these macro-horrors down to the intimate, suburban level. He proved, with stark authority, that the incomprehensible "Void" could manifest within the confines of a Los Angeles tract house, transforming the mundane into the terrifying and rendering domesticity itself a precarious bastion against an encroaching existential threat.

Thematic Anchor: The Fortified Cage

Matheson's architecture of dread is fundamentally built on post-war anxieties about Mass Conformity and the inherent fragility of the social contract. The construct of the Solvable Monster presents a profound paradox: the infected are a pathological phenomenon, a biological problem with a theoretical scientific solution. This grants the protagonist a degree of agency, a tangible enemy to research and combat, fostering a false sense of control. Yet, this very solvability engenders a deeper, more insidious horror: if the monster is "natural" and explicable by science, then Neville's systematic slaughter of them is not a holy crusade against evil, but a genocidal act against a new, biologically distinct species. The moral compass of the survivor splinters, irrevocably staining the hero's hands, revealing the Moral Rot inherent in desperate survival, a stark representation of Pillar B.

The horror of Conformity manifests in the vampire horde, a monolithic mass that moves with a single, unthinking purpose, tapping directly into the Cold War dread of the individual's dissolution into a systemic collective, a faceless mob stripped of individual will or identity, a terrifying echo of totalitarian states. This collective represents an inverse reflection of societal order —an unholy communion of the damned —further cementing Pillar B's concerns about the corruption of humanity—the Contamination of the Domestic marks a critical architectural evolution. While Toomer depicted the natural environment invading the sanctity of the home, Matheson renders the home itself as a Fortified Cage, a locus of siege. The suburban sanctuary, once a symbol of post-war prosperity and security, becomes a permanent site of nightly siege, a desperate barrier against an omnipresent threat. Every wall, every bolted door, every drawn curtain becomes a testament to a world irrevocably lost, trapping the individual in a state of perpetual, agonizing vigilance, a monument to a besieged interior world, a chilling manifestation of Pillar C's experimental psyche under duress.

Thematic Anchor: The Lovecraft Metric

Matheson stands as the critical translational architect who meticulously "earths" the cosmic collapse, rendering it comprehensible for the 20th century. Alien, incomprehensible laws governed Lovecraft's environmental horror; Epidemiological Laws rule Matheson's urban collapse, precise mechanisms of disease and adaptation, terrifying because of their scientific explicability. He took Lovecraft's profound "Existential Inadequacy," the sense of human insignificance before vast, indifferent forces, and applied it with surgical precision to a tangible, abandoned suburbia, transforming cosmic dread into the mundane terror of empty supermarkets and decaying homes.

The Ecstasy of Decay in Matheson's work manifests as the pathological body; it is not a cosmic dissolution of the spirit or mind, but a materialist simplification of Lovecraft's abstract, spiritual dissolution. The human organism is reduced to a mere host for a bacillus, a biological betrayal from within, aligning with Pillar A's external biological threat. Conceptual Chaos, in Matheson's paradigm, is sociological. The human mind breaks under the pressure of swapped definitions, where "human" and "monster" exchange attributes, creating an unbearable cognitive dissonance that eradicates prior moral frameworks, a direct assault on the experimental psyche, defining Pillar C. The Fantasy of Order, the inherent human impulse to impose meaning, receives a Nihilistic End. The individual is rendered utterly irrelevant to the emergence of a new order, proving with brutal finality that the human "system" is as fragile and transient as Lovecraft's concept of a "meaningless accident" in a vast, uncaring cosmos.

Richard Matheson provided the essential blueprint for the Modern Monster, meticulously transitioning the horror hegemony from Lovecraft's philosophical void and Toomer's atmospheric erasure to a narrative paradigm defined by scientific precision and personal devastation. He proved that the greatest horror was the inevitable Obsolescence of the Individual in the face of a new, conformist, and scientifically determined system. This obsolescence is a profound moral and psychological blow, touching both Pillar B, through the erosion of ethical frameworks, and Pillar C, dissolving the concept of individual selfhood. The structural legacy of this chapter is the creation of a vast, empty landscape in which the individual is under relentless siege. The architecture demands a further evolution: the next step in the hegemony must take this "Physical Siege" and intensify it into a "Communal Psychological Siege." The abject isolation of Robert Neville must transmute into the pervasive Group Paranoia of a trapped collective. The architect who accomplished this, converting the last man's profound solitude into the terrifying claustrophobia of the "Trapped Small Town," is Shirley Jackson. Matheson established the Scientific Siege; the hegemony would now explore Social Paranoia. The stage was thus irrevocably set for the advent of Shirley Jackson's masterful explorations of internal dissolution.

Chapter 24 Shirley Jackson: The Citadel of Domestic Malice

The terror of existence demands an accounting of the self, not merely of the external world. Richard Matheson's external apocalypse, characterized by its scientific parameters and global reach, yielded an insufficient prognosis for humanity's internal state; the subsequent horror hegemony pivoted violently inward, necessitating a precise diagnosis of the psychological collapse of the American individual. Shirley Jackson (1916–1965) emerged as the definitive architect of this crucial shift, moving the focus from the vast, empty landscape to the intimate, hostile community. Her architectural contribution systematically stripped horror of its conventional monsters and its external scientific explanations. Jackson unequivocally proved that the most terrifying threat is not the viral enemy outside the fortified door, but the insidious cruelty inherent in the human community and the relentless psychological siege waged within the seemingly sacred confines of the home. This profound shift irrevocably established the parameters for Pillar C (Experimental Psyche), detailing the meticulous deconstruction of the individual mind, and Pillar B (Moral Rot), exposing the profound ethical decay within societal structures. Jackson's work is a direct architectural handoff from Richard Matheson, converting his global, external plague into a localized, internal pathology, thereby adding the crucial wing of The Domesticated Nightmare to the burgeoning house of horror.

Thematic Anchor: The Sentient Mirror of Hill House

Jackson's core thematic anchor is the horror of isolation, psychological fragility, and the terrifying violence of conformity. She uses seemingly normal, domestic settings to reveal profound existential dread, dissecting the very fabric of communal and personal stability. The self contains the seeds of its own destruction, requiring only a fertile ground for cultivation, a concept vividly explored in *The Haunting of Hill House* (1959). This narrative gathers a small group to investigate a notoriously malevolent mansion. The protagonist, Eleanor Vance, a woman already burdened by an internalized legacy of guilt and an acute sense of worthlessness, becomes the primary, almost predestined target. The house does not manifest overt spectral entities; instead, it meticulously amplifies Eleanor's deep-seated guilt, her pervasive loneliness, and her profound psychological insecurity, systematically dismantling her sanity from within.

The central ambiguity remains absolute: whether the house possesses genuine supernatural agency or if Eleanor's psyche undergoes an autonomous and devastating disintegration. The house functions as a mirror, reflecting and distorting the inherent weaknesses of the human mind, then actively consuming them. This deliberate ambiguity cultivates an unanswerable dread, confirming the absolute vulnerability of consciousness itself and rendering the individual utterly defenseless against both internal and external pressures.

Thematic Anchor: The Banality of the Communal Ritual

Humanity possesses an inherent capacity for systematic, unthinking cruelty, formalized through tradition, a truth laid bare in "The Lottery" (1948). Here, horror manifests through the casual, unquestioning annual ritual of a small, ordinary American town. This communal ceremony culminates in a brutal stoning, an act of grotesque violence perpetrated by neighbors and family members against a randomly selected member of their own community. The narrative unequivocally reveals the terrifying, unexamined power of blind tradition and the suffocating force of social conformity, which permits and perpetuates atrocity under the guise of custom.

The participants execute their roles with a dispassionate normalcy, confirming the absolute erosion of individual moral agency. The story's horror resides in the chilling revelation that absolute evil requires no supernatural intervention, no monstrous antagonist; it resides within the collective human heart, ready to be unleashed through ritual and social pressure, rendering communal existence a perpetual threat. The desire for sanctuary can provoke the very malevolence it seeks to escape, as meticulously detailed in *We Have Always Lived in the Castle* (1962). In this narrative, the horror originates from the relentless siege and pervasive paranoia experienced by the Blackwood sisters. They are driven into absolute psychological isolation, a direct consequence of the ostracizing, curious, and ultimately hostile town that surrounds them. The external community, fueled by rumor, suspicion, and judgment, becomes an active, psychological antagonist, forcing the sisters into a hermetic, self-imposed existence. The narrative explores the complex, intertwined dynamics of familial loyalty and the crushing weight of public condemnation. This siege proves that a community's external gaze can construct a prison as impenetrable and terrifying as any physical edifice, confirming the individual's inescapable vulnerability to collective malice.

Thematic Anchor: The Post-War Suburban Prison

Jackson wrote primarily from her perspective as a suburban wife, a mother, and a keen observer of post-war American conformity. Her unique context provided the necessary experiential material for converting the vast, external horror into an intimate, domestic threat. The artificial constructs of societal order harbor a virulent psychological pathogen, a premise Jackson explored with unyielding precision. Jackson's literary career coincided with the rise of the American suburbs, the burgeoning consumer culture, and the immense, unspoken pressure for social conformity during the 1950s. This atmosphere of enforced order, superficial cheerfulness, and artificial domestic happiness constituted her primary artistic target.

She systematically subverted the myth of the safe, clean American community, transforming the suburban town and the seemingly normal domestic space—the house itself—into a terrifying, inescapable prison. Her works unequivocally declare that violence and cruelty are not anomalies but deeply embedded components within the everyday rituals and polite customs of American life, festering beneath a veneer of normalcy. This reveals the terrifying truth that the most oppressive forces reside not in distant lands but within the very fabric of one's immediate, supposedly idyllic environment, rendering escape an illusion. Jackson executed a crucial psychological handoff, reconfiguring the landscape of interior dread from that of her predecessors. The locus of terror shifts, but its fundamental psychological grip persists. Poe's terror often manifested through the unreliable narrator, whose internal decay served as the monstrous entity. Jackson externalized this psychological collapse, projecting it onto the house itself. Hill House, for example, is not merely haunted by external spirits but by the collective wickedness, the accumulated traumas, and the psychological needs of its past and present victims, becoming a sentient repository of human pathology.

Thematic Anchor: The Lovecraft Metric

Shirley Jackson provides the necessary antithesis to H.P. Lovecraft's cosmic scale. She meticulously shrinks the vast, philosophical dread into the contained psychological dread of the home, proving that terror is inversely proportional to its scope. Lovecraft's environmental horror encompasses cosmic, unknowable vastness; Jackson's cursed space is the meticulously contained, psychological, and domestic environment. Hill House is metaphysically hostile; it is inherently malevolent and communally infused with prior traumas, actively working against human sanity rather than merely reacting to it. Jackson thus applied Lovecraft's profound sense of existential inadequacy—the universe's utter indifference to human fate—to the singular, claustrophobic locus of the house, transforming external cosmic dread into internal structural pathology.

The decay of the spirit is more devastating than the corruption of the flesh, a concept central to Jackson's psychological decay, in contrast to Lovecraft's ecstasy of decay. Lovecraftian horror often sought an uncorporeal liberation; Jackson's psychological decay charts a different trajectory; her horror is not the decay of the body, but the systematic, total decay of the mind and the very self. The terror originates from the soul being devoured by its own accumulated history, its unexpiated guilt, and its inherent vulnerabilities, leaving only an empty husk of consciousness. This confirms that the most excruciating dissolution is the complete annihilation of the self. Jackson's communal chaos presents a starkly human equivalent; her logic is fundamentally sociological chaos. The greatest terror she evokes is the realization that human moral logic has failed utterly, as seen in the unthinking brutality of "The Lottery." This represents the secular equivalent of Dante's contrapasso, but indifferent neighbors apply it. The illusion of resolution offers false comfort against intractable suffering, a concept Jackson embodies in her unsolvable psychology, in direct opposition to Matheson's fantasy of order.

Shirley Jackson is the essential architect who definitively defined modern psychological and domestic horror, solidifying a new foundation for terror. She successfully transformed the external siege of the apocalypse, as presented by Matheson, into the internal siege of the self and the relentless psychological assault of the community. Her groundbreaking work established the enduring template in which the greatest horror resides not in the monstrous entity but in the devastating failure of the individual mind and the inherent, pervasive cruelty of the collective. This constitutes a pivotal moment in the architecture of dread, redirecting the very locus of fear. The hegemony now demands the next logical step in the escalating trajectory of terror. Jackson's meticulously constructed psychological siege requires infusion with the modern, urban paranoia that increasingly defined the 1960s. The quiet, small-town mob, with its ingrained traditions and casual malice, must be replaced by a terrifying, conspiratorial urban collective. The next architect must take Jackson's profoundly unsettling domestic setting and expand on it, exposing the terrifying possibility that the community's quiet cruelty is not merely traditional but an organized, pervasive, and profoundly evil conspiracy. The stage was thus irrevocably set for the transition from the Community Under Siege to the Covenant of the Unborn. The audit was moving from the small town to the high-rise. The time of the conspiracy had arrived, the baton passing to Ira Levin.

Chapter 25 Ira Levin: The Conspiratorial Home and the Erosion of Proximal Trust

The human mind, a labyrinthine construct of perception and memory, offered Shirley Jackson the perfect stage for psychological siege; her dread resided within the terrifying ambiguity of an internal landscape. The late 1960s, however, necessitated a radical architectural reorientation of this fundamental dread, demanding its translocation from the spectral confines of the "haunted" psyche to the tangible reality of the Urban Collective. Ira Levin (1929–2007) was the architect who executed this fusion precisely, melding Jackson's insidious domestic dread with the intense paranoia and systemic breakdowns permeating his contemporary society. Through the meticulously constructed narratives of *Rosemary's Baby* (1967) and *The Stepford Wives* (1972), Levin formalized the immutable structural blueprint of Domestic Conspiracy. He established the absolute truth that terror originates not from the ephemeral specter, but from the terrifying certainty that the individuals closest to one's being—spouse, physician, neighbors—comprise the highly organized, profoundly malevolent agents of one's inevitable destruction. This foundational architectural shift from internal disquiet to external, yet intimate, hostile construction anchors itself irrevocably within Pillar A: The Invasive Breach, operating through sacrosanct social contracts, corrupting the very concept of sanctuary.

Thematic Anchor: The Domestic Conspiracy

The architecture of human society rests upon the fragile, yet purportedly sacred, foundations of trust within institutions like marriage and medicine; Levin's corpus reveals the terrifying fragility of these constructs, positing the horror of Betrayal as a primordial, absolute force, and exposing the irretrievable collapse of confidence that constitutes Pillar B: The Symmetrical Debt. *Rosemary's Baby* meticulously dissects this rot, detailing the systematic psychological manipulations inflicted upon Rosemary Woodhouse by her immediate neighbors within The Bramford. The horror solidifies as a Contract of the Soul: her husband, Guy, has literally traded her reproductive autonomy, her very corporeal sovereignty, for a successful acting career, transforming her into a commodity within a nefarious transaction.

The neighbors operate as a highly organized occult corporation, their apparent benevolence a meticulously constructed facade for their heinous purpose, turning a residential building into a hermetically sealed laboratory for ritualistic sacrifice. *The Stepford Wives*, conversely, manifests a distinct, yet equally insidious, horror—the Gothic of the Suburbs—where Joanna Eberhart apprehends that the neighborhood men systematically murder their wives, replacing them with passive, robotic duplicates. This is no metaphor; it is a literal, mechanical re-engineering of human existence, with the "Monster" assuming the tangible form of unchecked male desire for total domestic control, expressed through clandestine technology. The idyllic suburban home, with its pristine facades, transforms into a mausoleum for individuality, each identical residence a cell in a vast, silent prison of conformity, a chilling monument to Pillar C: The Experimental Psyche.

Thematic Anchor: The Medicalization of the Occult

The mid-1960s to the early 1970s marked an era of profound societal upheaval, irrevocably defined by the ascent of Second-Wave Feminism and a pervasive erosion of public trust in established authority. Within this tumultuous context, Feminist Horror and Bodily Autonomy become central to Levin's clinical audit of the female experience within a rigidly patriarchal system. Rosemary is systematically gaslit by her husband and her obstetrician, Dr. Sapirstein; her legitimate fears and perceptions are pathologized, discrediting her internal reality. The horror solidifies as the Medicalization of the Occult—the insidious utilization of professional authority to mask a supernatural violation, transforming her body into a contested architectural site, meticulously prepared for an unspeakable tenant, a direct engagement with Pillar C.

Furthermore, the Urban/Suburban Transition represents a crucial architectural re-evaluation of the traditional "Gothic Trap." Levin demonstrably moved this insidious trap from the decaying, remote castle to the immediate, inescapable proximity of modern living; The Bramford functions as a vertical, layered prison, while the sterile, conformist suburb of Stepford becomes a sprawling, open-air asylum, its mundane appearances masking profound confinement and systemic surveillance. The Structural Handoff from Jackson is precise and deliberate: Levin absorbed Jackson's profound understanding of the "Banality of Evil" and provided it with a tangible Checklist, systematically expunging the "maybe" of the haunting, eliminating all ambiguity. By rendering the evil palpably real, externally organized, and meticulously planned, he structurally prepared the hegemony of horror for the inevitable arrival of the literal Devil.

Thematic Anchor: The Claustrophobia of Proximity

The systematic erosion of trust, an indispensable pillar of civilized existence, and the pervasive fear of invisible, corporate control form the foundational premise of Levin's architecture of dread, directly engaging Pillar A and Pillar B. The Betrayal of Marriage establishes the ultimate Gothic villain, not through overt monstrosity, but through quiet, insidious domestic treachery; the sanctified space of the home is definitively re-architected as the Primary Site of the Trap, a sealed chamber for the execution of a pre-determined fate, the conjugal bed itself an altar for profound violation. Concurrently, the Betrayal of Medicine, through the characterization of the doctor as a high priest of the coven, unleashes a direct, devastating assault upon societal reliance on modern science and professional authority.

Science, the purported bastion of reason, is revealed to be the perfect "veil"—an architectural camouflage—for ancient malice and diabolical intent, transforming the clinic into a ritual chamber. The Claustrophobia of Proximity, masterfully employed by Levin, uses the specific architectural dynamics of the modern apartment building and the suburban enclave to induce a unique, inescapable dread. The confinement is not physical distance; it is Psychological Proximity, where thin walls ensure neighbors are always listening, and shared spaces become zones of inescapable surveillance, fostering a pervasive, chilling sense of omnipresent threat, a direct deployment of Pillar C, as it weaponizes the immediate environment against mental fortitude.

Thematic Anchor: The Lovecraft Metric

Ira Levin provides the crucial, secularizing intermediary step for the Conspiracy genre, establishing a robust, rational framework for fear before the inevitable Theological Revival.

Environmental Horror, specifically "The Urban Hive," definitively characterizes Levin's "Cursed Space." Alien laws governed Lovecraft's environments; Levin's cursed space is the Modern Hive—the dense, interconnected apartment building or the seemingly idyllic suburb. The insidious conspiracy systematically contaminates both the public space and the private, intimate space, rendering sanctuary obsolete, with the architecture itself becoming an active, complicit participant in the systemic dread, an undeniable component of Pillar A.

The Ecstasy of Decay, concerning "The Occupied Body," marks a significant divergence and evolution. Lovecraft often explored "Uncorporeal Liberation," a transcendent release from the physical form; Levin, conversely, focuses with clinical precision on the Occupied Body, as Rosemary's body is not merely violated, but systematically appropriated, a biological vessel used by an external force. This materialist precursor to spiritual possession lays essential groundwork for the fully realized spiritual possession narratives seen in *The Exorcist*, establishing a clear lineage of architectural terror within Pillar C. Finally, the Fantasy of Order is completely subverted by Levin's stark portrayal of the Triumph of the System; the individual protagonist, despite moments of lucid realization, cannot fundamentally defeat the organized collective. This reinforces Lovecraftian fatalism: the "Great Old Ones" (or their human agents) always win, and the individual is architecturally crushed beneath the weight of an insurmountable, pre-ordained order.

Ira Levin stands as the essential architect of Paranoid and Domestic Conspiracy, his designs possessing an unnerving, clinical precision that reshaped the very foundations of modern horror. He successfully fused the psychological siege of the home with the urban, modern dread of systemic betrayal, proving that the true monster is a malevolent Social Contract signed in blood behind one's unsuspecting back. His profound contribution cemented the architectural blueprint of intimate, pervasive malevolence. The structural legacy of this chapter is the creation of a sophisticated, secular conspiracy framework, so meticulously detailed and chillingly plausible that it unequivocally required the return of the Explicit Supernatural to maximize the intensity of fear. Having thoroughly explored the horror of the Neighbor—the insidious, proximal human agent of evil—the evolving hegemony of horror now demanded the exploration of the horror of the Inhabitant—the demonic entity taking residence within the body itself. The next architect in this lineage must take Levin's modern, urban context and utilize it to re-establish the absolute reality of demonic possession. The stage was thus set for the transition from the Domestic Conspiracy to the Theological Invasion; the era of the spiritual occupant had surpassed that of the human agent. The blueprints were drawn for William Peter Blatty.

Chapter 26 William Peter Blatty: The Sanctum Undone: Architecture of Demonic Certainty

A profound structural exhaustion afflicted the horror hegemony by the late 1960s; its foundational edifices, once formidable, threatened collapse. Ira Levin (Chapter 25) constructed a universe governed by cynical human conspiracy, a cold, calculable dread. H.P. Lovecraft (Chapter 21) posited an ultimate truth of cosmic indifference, a vast, uncaring void. These pathways collectively excavated a profound vacuum in the architectural landscape of fear, where the spiritual element had been systematically expunged. Into this desolation stepped William Peter Blatty (1928–2017), the architect whose singular vision shattered the secular containment of the modern era. His genius revived the absolute, unforgiving theological terror of the Medieval Age. Blatty's seminal novel, *The Exorcist* (1971), violently reestablished the demonic as a scientifically verifiable reality, forcing the secular world to confront the absolute moral threat of Satanic invasion and anchoring horror firmly within Pillar B: The Symmetrical Debt, where the universe itself renders judgment upon transgression.

Thematic Anchor: The Failure of Secular Diagnostic Capability

The core thematic anchor of Blatty's architectural design is the horror of spiritual siege, a relentless assault upon the human soul; it stages an undeniable clash between the certainties of modern science and the absolute truth of theological evil. This narrative grounds itself in Blatty's meticulous research into a genuine 1949 case of demonic possession, granting its fictions the gravitas of documented reality. The invasion commences within the deceptive tranquility of a modern, academic, secular environment in Georgetown. Regan MacNeil, a twelve-year-old girl, becomes the victim, her innocence a vessel for profound corruption. Her symptoms are subjected to rigorous, systematic analysis by medical professionals. These experts ultimately fail to identify any pathology, their accumulated knowledge proving insufficient against the encroaching darkness.

This failure of the secular system forces a paradigm shift, compelling the diagnosis to transition from empirical science to ancient theology. The case is assigned to Father Damien Karras, a Jesuit priest and psychiatrist whose own struggles mirror the era's spiritual doubt. Karras's investigation confirms the supernatural nature of the possession through documented phenomena such as unknown languages, levitation, and dramatic temperature shifts. These events defy all materialist explanation, stripping away the comfort of rational thought. The ultimate confrontation manifests in the rite of exorcism, a spiritual battle conducted by Karras and

Father Lankester Merrin. The demon, Pazuzu, operates with malevolent intelligence, exploiting Karras's deepest fears and profound guilt. The exorcism culminates in success, yet this victory arrives at an immense, irredeemable cost: the lives of both priests. Karras, in an act of supreme moral sacrifice, physically draws the demon into his own body before tragically casting himself from a window.

Thematic Anchor: Documentary Realism as an Intellectual Weapon

William Peter Blatty conceived *The Exorcist* precisely at the zenith of the "God is Dead" movement. This intellectual landscape, characterized by theological uncertainty, rendered the perfect environment for his architectural intervention. Blatty's personal, unwavering faith, coupled with a rigorous commitment to documented reality, profoundly shaped his choice of subject matter. His biography reveals the precise blend of aptitudes: a former Catholic, a seasoned journalist, and a successful screenwriter. This allowed him to fuse forensic objectivity with theological understanding. The novel's structural integrity is built on Father Karras's intellectual struggle. Karras stands as the narrative's indispensable lens; he is educated, rational, and inherently skeptical.

The horror's absolute success derives from its presentation through the mind of this highly educated individual who is compelled by irrefutable facts to conclude the Devil is a real, active entity. Blatty's relentless commitment to "documentary realism" served as a powerful intellectual mechanism, convincing readers that the events depicted were not mere fantasies but verifiable phenomena. Blatty's work represents a pivotal Structural Handoff from Ira Levin. Blatty masterfully appropriated Levin's modern paranoia template, then executed a profound inversion of the source of evil. Blatty systematically replaced Levin's human conspiracy with a single, overwhelmingly powerful intelligence—Pazuzu. This shift cemented the horror firmly within Pillar B: The Symmetrical Debt, as the conflict centers on spiritual corruption and the soul's eternal fate.

Thematic Anchor: Possession as Spiritual Violation

Blatty's meticulously constructed architecture of dread relies fundamentally upon the recognition that modern science remains utterly insufficient to defend against fundamental, absolute evil. The novel systematically demolishes the perceived authority of secular institutions. The medical establishment exhausts every conceivable explanation for Regan's symptoms. This failure constitutes the foundational source of terror, confirming that the affliction is theological in nature. A profound crisis of logic ensues as the possession phenomena categorically defy all rational explanation. Blatty masterfully redirects the theme of bodily violation and transmutes it into a fundamentally spiritual desecration.

Possession functions as a visceral, spiritual rape; the demon's absolute control over Regan's adolescent body is depicted as a brutal, agonizing invasion. The defilement targets not merely the physical form, but aims precisely at blasphemy and the systematic destruction of innocence itself. Regan's grotesque physical state reintroduces the visceral aesthetic of Medieval horror, as found in Dante, directly into the modern home. The body becomes an undeniable battleground, a contested territory for the warring forces of God and Satan. Blatty's narrative directly challenges and overturns H.P. Lovecraft's core premise of cosmic indifference. By rendering the demon malicious and intimately concerned with human morality, Blatty unequivocally affirms that the universe is fundamentally moral and actively cares about human sin.

Thematic Anchor: The Lovecraft Metric

Blatty's *The Exorcist* stands as the definitive anti-Lovecraftian text, a profound philosophical counter-argument etched in terror. While both architects explore the boundaries of unknowable power, Blatty's work diametrically opposes Lovecraft's nihilism. In the realm of Environmental Horror, Lovecraft's cursed spaces resonate with an alien vastness; Blatty constructs a sacrificial space out of the mundane. The cursed space is precisely the modern secular home—a supposed sanctuary of domesticity and rational thought. Unlike Lovecraft's cosmos, Blatty's space becomes a concentrated battleground because the universe possesses an active concern for which moral force ultimately triumphs.

Regarding The Ecstasy of Decay, Lovecraft's vision sought Uncorporeal Liberation; Blatty treats the possessed body as a sacred vessel, an inviolable temple subjected to egregious invasion. Blatty unequivocally affirms the physical body as the site of meaningful moral conflict. Concerning Conceptual Chaos, Lovecraft's architecture shatters the mind with alien logic; Blatty offers theological certainty. The chaotic phenomena are not indications of an unhinged cosmos, but irrefutable proofs of an ancient, organized spiritual order. Finally, regarding The Fantasy of Order, Lovecraft's world offers no solace; Blatty restores a Moral Order. The horror is demonstrably defeatable through profound moral sacrifice and faith. The resolution is an unequivocal Moral Victory, restoring a sense of cosmic justice.

William Peter Blatty stands as the essential architect who definitively completed the revival of theological horror for the modern age. His singular achievement lies in subjecting demonic possession to a systematic scientific gauntlet, thereby legitimizing the supernatural threat within an era of secularism. His seminal novel provided the absolute blueprint for contemporary theological horror, offering an alternative vision of a universe where morality holds ultimate sway. The horror hegemony, having witnessed the re-establishment of these profound spiritual truths, now demands the construction of the Commercial Apex. The intricate psychological dread cultivated by Blatty and the powers of a revived supernatural threat must now be synthesized into a single, universally accessible format that dominates the global market. The subsequent architects are tasked with taking these profound themes and scaling them to a massive, generational form. This next crucial stage is characterized by the Banal Apocalypse, paving the way for the inevitable crowning of the undisputed King of Horror. The structural audit moved from the specific room of Regan MacNeil to the sprawling town of Jerusalem's Lot. But first, we need to discuss the diaspora of the coming age.

Chapter 27 The Interregnum: The Great Synthesis and the Sovereignty of the Living Dark

The descent from the theological desecration of William Peter Blatty into the mid-1970s represents the most violent structural pivot in the history of the Unbroken Chain. It marks the absolute moment when the Gothic ceased to be a genre of the "Distant Other"—the monk in the medieval cellar, the scientist in the isolated lab, or the count in the crumbling castle—and became the very atmosphere of the immediate. By the dawn of this era, the "Monster" had been systematically hunted out of the monasteries and the morgues, forced into a final, terminal fusion within the American capillaries. The Hegemony demanded a synthesis where the systemic, the biological, and the psychological collapsed into a singular, unified state of existence. Into this high-pressure void stepped three sovereigns who did not merely write books; they curated our collective collapse. They are the architects of the Everyman Gothic, the Pathological Breach, and the Temporal-Biological Cage.

Thematic Anchor: The Temporal-Biological Cage

Standing as the unwavering axis of this era is the "Queen of the Breach," Octavia Butler. To read Butler—specifically the visceral, time-shredding agony of *Kindred*—is to undergo a clinical audit of the soul that no predecessor possessed the courage to contemplate. She seized the "Systemic Trap" of Séjour and the "Ancestral Memory" of Hopkins and proved that history is not a ghost to be exorcised through ritual, but a physical gravity. In her hands, the Gothic became a metabolic necessity: a literal, cellular pull that drags the body back through the screaming throat of time to the site of its own ancestral undoing. Butler taught us that the "Self" is a legal fiction; the only truth is the Genetic Debt. She transformed the genre into a laboratory in which power is an inescapable parasite and survival is a form of grinding trauma. Her work redefined the Pillar of Systemic Injustice by removing the distance between the victim and the history of their oppression.

In Butler's architecture, the past is not behind us; it is a predator waiting in our DNA. The weight of her contribution lies in her refusal to allow the Gothic to remain a fantasy. By grounding the "Haunted House" in the historical reality of the plantation, she effectively dismantled the comfort of the "Ghost Story." The ghosts in Butler's world do not rattle chains; they exert a temporal suction that forces the modern protagonist to inhabit the physical pain of their forebears. This is the Temporal-Biological Cage, a structure whose walls are made of time and whose bars are made of blood. She proved that the "Systemic Monster" is a self-sustaining loop of historical trauma that requires the body as fuel. It is a terrifying advancement of the

Moral Pillar, shifting the focus from individual sin to collective, historical culpability.

Thematic Anchor: The Everyman Gothic

Flanking this legacy is Stephen King, the man who finally and irrevocably "Earthed" the nightmare. He took the "Conceptual Chaos" of Lovecraft and the "Domestic Paranoia" of Levin and planted them in the nutrient-rich, blood-soaked soil of the American Everyman. King realized that a haunted vehicle, a psychic child, or a rabid dog served as a more potent conductor for the "Living Dark" than any ancient count, because these monsters inhabit the exact rooms where we love, sleep, and inevitably fail. King's genius lay in his ability to weaponize the Mundane. He proved that the most terrifying sound in the universe is not a demonic howl, but the rhythmic heartbeat of a neighbor you realized too late you never truly knew.

He is the undisputed master of the "Social Interior," localizing the Moral Rot of the old world into the suburban lawns and school hallways of the new. His architecture is one of "Invasive Familiarity," in which the safety of the domestic is revealed as a fragile, thin layer stretched over a bottomless pit. King's structural contribution is the Democratization of Dread. He moved the Gothic from the elite intellectual sphere into the blue-collar consciousness. In his work, the "Cursed Object" is a 1958 Plymouth Fury; the "Ancient Evil" is a shapeshifter in a sewer pipe that feeds on the specific, local fears of a small town. This shift forces the reader to acknowledge that the Hegemony is not "out there" in the cosmos, but "down here" in the grocery store. King ensured that the distance of the fantastical would never again break the Unbroken Chain.

Thematic Anchor: The Pathological Breach

Parallel to him, Dean Koontz emerged as the architect of the Pathological Breach. He took the "Scientific Hubris" of Shelley and the "Chemical Duality" of Stevenson and accelerated them into the high-velocity paranoia of the modern techno-thriller. Koontz's horror is defined by the terror of the "Optimized Body" and the scientific anomaly—the byproduct of a laboratory that challenges the very sanctity of the human blueprint. He fused the electronic suspense of the modern age with a focus on the individual's defiance of systemic erasure. Koontz addressed the Experimental Psyche by grounding it in the terrifying possibilities of biotechnology and the clandestine reach of government.

His work explores the "Breach of the Natural," where the monster is a hyper-intelligent mistake, a biological asset gone rogue. The Pathological Breach is a response to the Atomic Age and the rise of the Surveillance State. In Koontz's architecture, the "Vampire" is replaced by the "Genetic Experiment," and the "Witch" is replaced by the "Telepathic

Project." This secularization of horror serves a vital purpose: it makes the threat Systemic and Material. If the monster is a product of a lab, then the monster is a product of the government and the corporation. This creates a state of Techno-Paranoia, where the tools of advancement become the instruments of extinction. Koontz's protagonists are often the "Common Man" forced into an asymmetrical war against a technological evil, reinforcing the Systemic Pillar while reflecting the acceleration of the late 20th century.

Thematic Anchor: The Lovecraft Metric

These architects represent a rare hegemonic phenomenon: sovereigns who provided the Great Synthesis. In this modern apex, the Systemic Pillar, re-engineered by Butler, no longer relies on legal documents; it is now a temporal predator. The horror is that your lineage is your sentence. The Moral Pillar, refined by King, has moved from the "Ancient Curse" to the "Domestic Rot." Evil is an infection in the community—the social contract being shredded by the very people sworn to uphold it. Finally, the Psychological and Biological Pillar, as expanded by Koontz, addresses the "Anxiety of the Synthetic." It is the fear that we are no longer "natural" beings, but "material" that can be edited and discarded.

This is the state of the Unbroken Chain as we enter the final chapters. The sovereigns have spoken, and the architecture is complete. We are no longer building a house; we are inhabiting a world where the Living Dark is the only permanent resident. Octavia Butler weaponized history as a biological trap and defined the body as a site of temporal debt. Stephen King democratized dread and localized the nightmare within the mundane, transforming the Gothic into a blue-collar mythology. Dean Koontz fused techno-paranoia with mutation, making the lab as terrifying as the tomb. The structural audit is now finalized; the ancient handoffs have culminated in a reality where the architecture of fear is indistinguishable from the architecture of life. The Unbroken Chain has coiled around the modern world, and the final accounting is at hand.

Chapter 28 Stephen King: The Banal Apocalypse: A Doctrine of Profane Irruption

The epochal shift in the mid-20th century posed a formidable structural challenge: the imperative to integrate the cosmic indifference of Lovecraft, the introspective terror of Poe, and the re-established supernatural certainty of Blatty into a singularly accessible, commercially dominant narrative form. The preeminent architect who definitively resolved this dilemma and thereby established the fundamental blueprint for the contemporary horror market was Stephen King. King codified The Banal Apocalypse, a doctrine that defines horror as the sudden, terrifying breakdown of the American quotidian. His singular contribution renders the cosmic and the traumatic profoundly accessible, unequivocally demonstrating that the most profound terrors flourish within the most unremarkable settings. This phenomenon represents a Pillar C: The Experimental Psyche contribution, as King's work fundamentally re-engineered the psychological mechanisms of dread for a mass audience.

Thematic Anchor: The Profane Irruption

Philosophical premise dictates that true terror lies not in the exotic, but in the violation of the assumed mundane; it is the insidious revelation that the fabric of reality, particularly within the perceived safety of domesticity, is inherently porous to malevolent forces. King's primary thematic anchor is the brutal confrontation between the American Everyman—the schoolteacher, the itinerant writer, the small-town police officer—and an ancient, immense, often Lovecraftian evil. This structural invasion of the everyday defines his oeuvre; his narratives focus unequivocally on the sudden, catastrophic invasion of a secluded, ordinary setting.

In *Carrie* (1974), the horror erupts with primordial force from the suffocating isolation and oppressive religious fanaticism of a domestic setting. In *The Shining* (1977), the supernatural siege is meticulously confined to a single domestic space, the Overlook Hotel, mirroring and accelerating the collapse of the nuclear family unit within its haunted corridors. His signature work, *The Stand* (1978), presents a literal apocalypse, an absolute societal collapse meticulously engineered by a superflu virus, elevating Matheson's epidemiological dread to a massive, continental battle between nascent good and absolute evil. *It* (1986) serves as the grand fusion of horror, featuring an ancient, shapeshifting entity that draws its immense power from cosmic fear, a direct inheritance from Lovecraft, while the characters' struggles are deeply psychological and communal, echoing the introspective anxieties of Poe and the shared dread of Jackson. King's narrative resolutions, while delivering climactic confrontation, frequently deny the facile purification characteristic of the Gothic. However, the specific monstrous manifestation is usually vanquished, the underlying source of evil is often cosmic, ancient, or demonstrably cyclical, a chilling suggestion that the terror will inevitably return, dormant but never truly defeated.

Thematic Anchor: The Everyman and the Market Apex

The architect's personal context is inextricably rooted in the American working class and the profound cultural shifts of the late 20th century, rendering his immense market dominance a structural event in the annals of horror literature. King emerged from difficult circumstances in Maine, a locale that became the perennial backdrop for his fiction, imbuing his narratives with the authentic voice of the American Everyman. This populist resonance rendered his protagonists—and his monsters—instantly relatable, blurring the lines between reader and victim. King represents the commercial apex, the figure who fundamentally transformed horror into a mass-market commercial genre, his unprecedented success forging the blueprint for today's independent, self-published authors and irrevocably proving horror's capacity for universal appeal.

His literary synthesis is an openly acknowledged debt to the entire established hegemony, meticulously integrating the unreliable narrator of Poe, the cosmic scale of Lovecraft, the tyrannical institution of Blatty, and the corrupted domesticity of

Jackson into his signature, sprawling narratives. King's horror is deeply rooted in contemporary trauma and personal struggles; novels such as *The Shining* and *Cujo* unsparingly explore the horror of addiction and the pervasive failure of the male protagonist, externalizing internal psychological decay into tangible monstrous forms. The normalization of the supernatural constitutes a critical structural element; King's monsters appear in laundromats, drainpipes, and average American cars, reinforcing the chilling theme that the terrifying is perpetually close to home, merely lurking beneath the veneer of the ordinary. This architectural approach grounds the cosmic into the commonplace, a Pillar B: The Symmetrical Debt revelation that societal and personal failures invite ancient evils.

Thematic Anchor: The Small Town as a Cursed Organism

King's meticulously constructed architecture of dread is founded on late-20th-century anxieties about communal stability, the inherent fragility of the social contract, and the inevitable return of the repressed past. His primary setting, the small American town, functions as a secular replacement for the Gothic castle, a microcosm where collective evil festered. The town itself often becomes the monster, cursed not by a singular ancestral transgression, but by a generational, systemic evil; the horror is that the community is either actively complicit in the malevolence or passively ignorant of its insidious presence, a fusion of Jackson's communal dread with a supernatural, external cause. King frequently employs childhood trauma and repressed memories as a potent mechanism of dread; the terror is the necessary confrontation with the dark, unspeakable secrets that the community buried decades ago, demanding their violent resurgence.

This represents a Pillar A: The Invasive Breach influence, as the external communal structure becomes the agent of torment. King successfully resolved the problem of scale that Lovecraft's work often presented, grounding the cosmic. He introduced entities of immense cosmic power, such as Pennywise the Clown, who functions as an avatar of an interdimensional being. Yet, he grounded this Lovecraftian scale in the accessible, primal image of the monster under the bed or lurking in the sewer. King also re-establishes the moral stakes revived by Blatty; his conflicts are frequently framed as absolute battles between good and evil, often incorporating elements of Biblical structure and explicit theological conflict, imbuing the horror with profound ethical weight.

Thematic Anchor: The Lovecraft Metric

Stephen King unequivocally represents the commercial synthesis of the entire horror hegemony. He successfully popularized the profound terror themes of Lovecraft by rendering them accessible and emotionally available to a mass audience. Regarding environmental horror, King's cursed town constitutes the systemic, generational contamination of the American small town. He grounds Lovecraft's idea of an ancient, sleeping, vast evil beneath a small-town locale like Derry; the environment is metaphysically hostile because it is built atop a psychic, non-human entity.

About the ecstasy of decay, Lovecraft sought Uncorporeal liberation. King's body functions primarily as a vessel for intense emotional pain and trauma; the physical horror is intensely visceral—telekinetic destruction, biological plague—but it serves the primary purpose of externalizing psychological suffering. Lovecraft's conceptual chaos shatters the mind with alien, incomprehensible logic. King's accessible chaos is a powerful fusion; he affirms Lovecraft's theme that the monster operates on alien rules, while giving the human characters the mental tools to partially understand and actively fight the chaos. The chaos is present, but it is rendered manageable by human bonds of friendship and love. Finally, concerning the fantasy of order, King's fantasy of heroism fundamentally rejects Lovecraft's ultimate nihilism. While King's evil is often cosmic, the human defense—friendship, love, sacrifice—always possesses genuine efficacy. The narrative resolution consistently provides a satisfying emotional conclusion, representing the triumph of the Everyman hero, the ultimate redemptive fantasy of order in a world threatened by the absolute.

Stephen King completed the commercial and thematic synthesis of the modern horror hegemony. He combined psychological trauma (Poe/Jackson) and existential threat (Lovecraft/Matheson) to create the definitive template for the Banal Apocalypse. His success legitimized horror as a major commercial genre and provided the foundational blueprint that independent and self-published authors use today to structure their narratives. The prevailing hegemony, however, requires one final structural step. King mastered the long, sweeping epic, often culminating in moral or emotional victory. The market, conversely, requires a definitive master of the efficient, technological thriller that provides a clear, rational, and ultimately controllable threat. The next architect must perfect the counter-narrative to King's moral epic: the horror of scientific conspiracy, where the individual hero employs pure intellect to defeat the evil system. This imperative leads us to the final structural pillar of contemporary dread. The audit of the American Everyman was complete; the audit of the Optimized System was beginning. The blueprints passed from the small town to the high-tech laboratory. The sovereign of the technological breach was ascending. Few have done it better than Dean Koontz.

Chapter 29 Dean Koontz: The Engineer of Contained Dread

The vast, emotive architectural expanse carved by Stephen King established a definitive mastery of the Banal Apocalypse. It perfected the emotional epic, yet its very success created a discernible structural void, necessitating a counter-narrative founded upon explicit rationality and a comprehensible locus of dread. Dean Koontz, born in 1945, emerged as the final essential architect to define the immediate modern era, his specialization fixed upon high-tension, scientifically explicable, and ultimately solvable horror. Koontz precisely codified The Technological Nightmare, thereby establishing the fundamental archetype of the Controllable Threat. He enacted a deliberate, intellectual rejection of the inherent nihilism propounded by Lovecraft and the cyclical, often inescapable tragedy woven by King; Koontz instead furnished incontrovertible proof that the individual hero, when fortified by intellect and an unwavering moral compass, possesses the immutable capacity to defeat even the most pervasive and insidious evil system. This fundamental premise anchors a distinct wing within the architectural edifice of terror, a chamber where the chaos of the unknown yields to the order of the knowable, where despair capitulates to agency, thereby constructing a unique narrative sanctuary from the boundless and the absurd.

Thematic Anchor: The Triumph of Disciplined Reason

The core thematic anchor in Koontz's structural design posits the triumph of human agency and disciplined reason over systemic malevolence, which is invariably engineered through scientific means. This philosophical stance affirms the Enlightenment ideal that humanity possesses the inherent capacity to understand and master its challenges, regardless of their seeming complexity. His protagonists, often ordinary individuals—teachers, writers, or simple craftspeople—find themselves inexorably drawn into extraordinary conspiracies, their mundane existences shattered by forces operating with clandestine efficiency. The horror presented in Koontz's oeuvre is rooted profoundly in scientific conspiracy, manifesting frequently through bio-technology, opaque military programs, or clandestine government experiments that have catastrophically unraveled.

Consider *Watchers* (1987); the primordial threat originates directly from a government laboratory, a testament to human hubris. This facility breeds a hyper-intelligent, genetically engineered golden retriever named Einstein and its terrifying, murderous counterpart, The Outsider, a creature of pure, destructive instinct. The dread here is not cosmic, but terrestrial, a product of human hands and fallible intellect, thus firmly placing the structural foundation within Pillar C: The Experimental Psyche, where the terror is an artifact of audacious scientific endeavor. Koontz seamlessly fused the psychological horror inherent to the genre with the thriller's relentless pace and acute suspense. This amalgamation creates narratives centered on an incessant pursuit, in which the protagonist is compelled to deploy every faculty of intellect and cunning to solve problems and expose and dismantle the intricate conspiracy, thereby averting a more widespread catastrophe. The optimistic ending features an invariable moral victory: the individual hero survives, the technological threat is contained with absolute finality, and the ethical order of the universe is reaffirmed as a foundational principle.

Thematic Anchor: The Post-Watergate Miasma

Dean Koontz's emergence during the 1970s and 1980s positioned him at a pivotal historical juncture, where he meticulously carved a distinct narrative niche rooted in unrelenting suspense, plausible science, and a steadfast affirmation of Christian morality. This specific cultural and philosophical context profoundly shaped the modern suspense-horror model he constructed. Koontz's career unfolded against a backdrop of pervasive public skepticism concerning governmental authority and the unchecked potential of technological power—a direct legacy of the Cold War's clandestine machinations and the profound societal paranoia ignited by events such as Watergate in the 1970s. This external milieu forms Pillar A: The Invasive Breach. It fostered a cultural readiness for narratives exploring institutional malevolence and the misuse of scientific advancement.

Koontz embraced the scientific narrative framework first established by Shelley and Stevenson, but he critically reframed the definitive source of evil. His threats are never uncontrollable cosmic entities; instead, they are invariably flawed human systems—corrupt government agencies, ethically compromised scientists, or avaricious corporate entities. This deliberate choice renders the "monster" defeatable, contingent upon the hero's capacity to unravel the intricate technical puzzle that defines its existence. Koontz meticulously fashioned a deliberate counter-narrative to King's horror, positioning his work as a direct architectural riposte. Where King's evil is often presented as cosmic, ancient, and generationally pervasive, Koontz's evil is local, contemporary, and conspiratorial. This profound duality—King embodying the sprawling emotional epic and Koontz perfecting the taut technological thriller—defined the horror landscape for several decades.

Thematic Anchor: The Contained Threat and the Rational Investigator

Koontz's distinctive architecture of dread is founded upon the very post-Watergate anxieties that permeated the public consciousness: governmental conspiracy and the unforeseen risks of bio-technological overreach. He transformed the Gothic theme of the "hidden secret" into a thoroughly modern, corporate, or governmental conspiracy. The structural genius of Koontz resides in the concept of the contained threat; his horrors are invariably confined within sterile laboratories, encrypted classified military files, or the opulent, insulated domains of wealthy, shadowy organizations. The horror itself does not emanate from the monster's inherent power, but rather from the human system actively protecting it, perpetuating its existence, and concealing its atrocities. This deliberate structural choice ensures the threat remains manageable and ultimately solvable.

Koontz also popularized the extensive use of bio-technological monsters—genetically engineered animals, super-viruses, and clones—integrating these contemporary anxieties into the fast-paced, relentless narrative. The dread arises not from supernatural intervention but from the deliberate manipulation of life itself, underscoring Pillar C, where human ambition creates its own monsters. Koontz's work further refines the pervasive themes of paranoia and betrayal established by Ira Levin, yet provides a crucial inversion of

Levin's cynical conclusions. While Levin's protagonists frequently succumb, Koontz's protagonists invariably achieve victory, dismantling the conspiracy through the application of intellect and sheer will. The Koontz protagonist stands as the ultimate evolution of the rational investigator, a direct descendant of Pliny and Van Helsing, proving that reason and unwavering courage constitute reliable defenses against systemic evil.

Thematic Anchor: The Lovecraft Metric

Dean Koontz provides the ultimate rationalist counter-thesis to the profound nihilism espoused by Lovecraft. Koontz's unwavering structural commitment to a solvable world fundamentally affirms the intrinsic value of human agency. Lovecraft's environmental horror established a vast, alien, and cosmologically indifferent space; Koontz's, in stark contrast, is local, technologically contaminated, and, crucially, temporary. The source of evil is typically a sterile, hidden environment, a direct consequence of human arrogance. The evil is rigorously contained, and the world existing outside the immediate sphere of the conspiracy invariably remains morally sound and redeemable.

Lovecraft famously sought Uncorporeal Liberation, an ecstasy of decay where the physical body dissolves into formless chaos. Koontz's technological body presents horror as the technological alteration of the form—genetic engineering or mutation. The threat here is inherently material and, significantly, scientifically reversible. The body's original integrity can be restored through the hero's intellect, providing a final affirmation of the scientific model when wielded for good. Lovecraft's Conceptual Chaos aimed to shatter the human mind with alien, non-Euclidean logic; Koontz's universe operates with utterly solvable logic. The phenomena, no matter how terrifying, adhere to knowable scientific rules. The logic is predicated upon the truth that the world remains fundamentally comprehensible and thus amenable to human intervention. Koontz's horror is, by its very design, solvable. He provides the ultimate Fantasy of Order for the modern era.

Dean Koontz completes a crucial structural link within the foundational hegemony of horror architects. He furnished the necessary counter-thesis to the moral and cosmic chaos that defined the latter half of the 20th century. By mastering the intricate contours of The Technological Nightmare and committing to the paradigm of the Controllable Threat, Koontz decisively defined the rationalist end of the horror spectrum. He proved that horror could operate as a powerful narrative force while simultaneously affirming the ultimate triumph of human intellect and moral agency. The hegemony of these foundational architects now stands complete. The legacy of King, who crafted the emotional epic, and Koontz, who engineered the rational thriller, established the two primary models of commercial horror that serve as blueprints for all subsequent writers. These two towering figures delineate the boundaries of modern popular horror, each offering a distinct pathway into the heart of dread. The structural audit was complete. The Unbroken Chain had successfully moved from the Juridical Specter of the Roman past to the Optimized Experiment of the digital future, but some fears don't have timelines.

Chapter 30 Octavia Butler: The Biological Covenant: A Doctrine of Systemic Entrapment and the Architecture of the Inescapable Self

The structural evolution of late 20th-century horror demanded a radical audit of the Gothic tradition; this audit necessitated a framework capable of bridging the ancestral trauma of the 19th-century slave narrative with the burgeoning speculative biological anxieties of the future. This imperative called for an architect who could render historical suffering not as a mere echo, but as a living, inescapable genetic inheritance. The preeminent architect who definitively resolved this profound historical and biological dissonance, thereby establishing the precise blueprint for "Systemic Dread," was Octavia Butler (1947–2006). Butler codified The Biological Covenant, a foundational doctrine defining horror as the inescapable entrapment of the individual within an interwoven matrix of power, genetics, and historical debt; this framework presents suffering as a self-replicating design. This covenant posits that individual agency operates within a pre-determined scaffold of inherited predispositions and external pressures; escape remains an illusion. This work represents a crucial Pillar A (External/Systemic) contribution, as Butler's architectural designs fundamentally re-engineered horror into a searing critique of biological and social hierarchy. Concurrently, it enacts a Pillar C (Experimental Psyche) influence, dissecting the psychological capitulation and adaptation demanded by such omnipresent, pervasive systems.

Thematic Anchor: The Temporal-Biological Cage

A central philosophical premise dictates that true terror lies not in a sudden irruption of the supernatural, but in the Inevitability of the System itself; it is the chilling revelation that the body is not a sanctuary of the sovereign self, but a site of negotiation, parasitism, and relentless historical claim. This absolute truth asserts that the body remains a battleground, a living archive of past violences and future obligations. In *Kindred* (1979), the horror manifests as a relentless Temporal Gravity, a physical law of consequence; Dana is dragged back through time to a 19th-century slave plantation by the genetic demand of her own ancestor. The haunting is literalized as an unbreakable biological and historical tether that ignores her agency, negating any illusion of personal freedom.

The body itself becomes a portal, a physical manifestation of historical debt, compelling her return to the source of trauma whenever her oppressor's lineage requires protection. In *Fledgling* (2005), Butler subverts the vampire mythos by reframing it as a study in Symbiotic Co-dependence and racialized biology, where horror resides in the profound loss of autonomy inherent in parasitic relationships. Her seminal

Xenogenesis trilogy (1987–1989) presents the ultimate Gothic invasion: the Oankali "save" humanity from self-destruction by forcibly merging with its genetic code, imposing a biological imperative of hybridization that fundamentally redefines humanity and its future. Butler's narrative resolutions deny the redemptive triumph of the Everyman hero; instead, they offer a Tragic Compromise in which survival requires the permanent surrender of the original self.

Thematic Anchor: The Pathological Reality of Power

The architect's personal context is fundamentally rooted in the intersection of the Black American experience and the cold, speculative rigor of science fiction. Growing up in a marginalized environment, Butler observed the invisible machinations of power and the "exquisite trauma" inherent in survival within oppressive social architecture; she transmuted this directly into her literary constructs. Butler represents the Intellectual and Systemic Apex, transforming horror into an incisive tool for auditing the social contract. Her literary synthesis integrates the systemic traps of Séjour, the ancestral memory of Hopkins, and the biological anxieties of Shelley into an uncompromising realism.

Butler's horror is rooted in the Pathological Reality of Power; her novels explore "compulsory intimacy"—the dehumanizing ways individuals are forced to love, serve, or merge with the systems that oppress them, such as forced procreation or inescapable bonds of dependence. The normalization of the Unthinkable constitutes her critical structural element; Butler's horrors appear in blood, the womb, and the family tree, reinforcing the chilling theme that the terrifying is the very foundation upon which the veneer of civility is built. This represents a profound Pillar B (Moral Rot) contribution, illustrating how systemic evils corrupt the individual and societal psyche from within, fundamentally altering moral landscapes and enforcing complicity through the very act of survival.

Thematic Anchor: The Anatomy of Systemic Siege

Butler's meticulously constructed architecture of dread is founded upon anxieties regarding Bodily Autonomy, the ethics of hierarchy, and the crushing weight of history. Her primary setting is the Inescapable Environment—whether the antebellum South or a post-apocalyptic wasteland—where human ethics are stripped to their bare essentials. The "Monster" in Butler's work is rarely a singular entity; it is the Hierarchy itself, a palpable force that dictates the terms of existence through institutionalized control and biological imperatives. The horror is that the community—and the protagonist—must participate in their own subjugation to ensure species continuity, a Faustian bargain with existence.

This represents a definitive Pillar A influence, where the external structure operates as a sentient, parasitic force. Butler resolved the problem of Lovecraftian scale by relocating the "immense and uncaring" from the cosmic void to the intimate domains of the Sociological and the Biological; her horrors are not of eldritch entities beyond human comprehension, but of systems and genetic programs that are all too comprehensible and intimately oppressive. Her aliens and vampires are masters of bureaucratic and genetic control, operating with a cold, rational logic that imbues their actions with chilling efficacy. This re-establishes the stakes of horror: the conflict is a complex struggle between Resistance and Assimilation, imbuing the horror with profound ethical weight.

Thematic Anchor: The Lovecraft Metric

Octavia Butler unequivocally represents the Systemic Synthesis of the entire horror hegemony. She popularized the themes of the "Lost Self" by rendering them as biological and historical facts; the self is not merely lost to existential angst but is literally altered or genetically redefined by an external system. Regarding environmental horror, Butler's Cursed Land is the Inescapable History of the Body itself; she grounds the idea of a vast evil not in a geographical location, but in a Covenant of Genetics. The environment is hostile because the protagonist's body is "owned" by the space's history.

About the ecstasy of decay, Butler rejected spiritual transcendence; her architecture posits the body as a site of Forced Evolution, where physical modification is a terrifying pathway to survival. Physical horror—loss of limbs, merging of DNA—demonstrates that the Self is a fluid, vulnerable, and negotiable construct. Butler makes the body's inevitable transformation intellectually devastating, forcing a re-evaluation of what constitutes humanity. Where Lovecraft's conceptual chaos shatters the mind with alien logic, Butler's chaos is a Hierarchy of Logic; she affirms that the Monster operates according to rational but utterly dehumanizing rules. Finally, her resolutions reject the Redemptive Hero; her characters survive by evolving into something no longer human. The triumph is the agonizing Endurance of the Victim within the system—a sobering Fantasy of Order where the covenant is written in blood and flesh.

Octavia Butler completed the systemic and biological synthesis of the modern horror hegemony. She integrated historical trauma and the existential threat posed by the biological Other to create the definitive template for Systemic Entrapment. Her work legitimized horror as a tool for profound social and biological audit, providing a foundational blueprint for authors who explore the Body as a Battlefield. The Unbroken Chain had moved through the halls of history and the laboratories of science to arrive at the cellular core of the individual. The structural audit was now complete, and the architects had finished their work. The narrative was no longer a question of construction, but one of recording the inevitable. The hegemony had evolved into a living document—a real-time audit of the hidden gems carving new dimensions into the existing edifice. The Unbroken Chain had completed its 2,000-year cycle. The time for the traditional Architects was over.

Chapter 31: The Modern Inheritance—The Cartography of Contemporary Terrors: The Perpetual Recalibration of Terror's Blueprint

The exhaustive journey through the Foundational Hegemony, a profound cartography traced across architects spanning from the precise bureaucratic anxieties of the Juridical Specter (Pliny) to the incomprehensible vastness of the Cosmic Apex (Lovecraft) and the democratized horrors of the Commercial Apex (King/Koontz), now reaches its formal completion. This tracing has laid bare the immutable laws that govern the very architecture of fear itself, revealing its unyielding mechanics. It reveals the primal blueprints, etched instructions within human consciousness, demonstrating that terror is an inherent structural component of our existence, perpetually available for calibrated manipulation. The consciousness is a palimpsest, its deepest layers inscribed with mechanisms of dread, awaiting the architect's precise touch.

Thematic Anchor: The Perpetual Recalibration

This chapter marks the formal termination of historical chronology as the primary analytical lens; it signifies a shift in epistemic inquiry. Our focus transcends the mere evolution of terror's forms and moves decisively towards the strategic deployment and meticulous recalibration of pre-existing terror structures. The Hegemony's foundational elements are living, malleable components. The thesis remains absolute: every successful contemporary horror narrative is a direct heir to an established historical blueprint; the concept of a "new" fear is a delusion. There exists only the highly calibrated application of the Hegemony's established laws, a systematic repurposing of humanity's primordial anxieties.

The transition from individual authorial study to the comprehensive discipline of Structural Archetype Analysis confirms human terror as a finite, perfectly engineered mechanism. This contemporary era is characterized by the high-pressure fusion of Stephen King's emotional accessibility (The Banal Apocalypse), Dean Koontz's relentless scientific efficiency (The Technological Nightmare), and the critical Systemic Synthesis established by Octavia Butler. These three towering figures do not invent; they delineate the absolute boundaries of modern horror, ensuring every new architect builds upon land already cleared by the enduring Hegemony.

Pillar A: The Visceral Thriller (The Pathological Breach)

This pillar inherits the mandate for explicit, high-pace conflict, first established by Matthew Gregory Lewis and weaponized by Dean Koontz. Lewis charted the topography of explicit torment, daring to render physical degradation with clarity. Koontz refined the precise mechanics of assault, often employing biologically engineered threats as instruments of calibrated terror, turning the body into a scientific experiment in distress. His creations are laboratories of fear where the human organism is merely a data point in the calculus of pain.

The structural mandate for Pillar A centers on the Pathological Breach—a biological or systemic anomaly that demands immediate, visceral confrontation. This architecture utilizes the Optimized Body as its primary tool and the Controllable Threat as its antagonist. However, this pillar incorporates Octavia Butler's Biological Covenant, asserting the human body as a site of systemic power and inherited vulnerability. The horror thus transpires as the agonizing realization of an inherent, inherited vulnerability encoded within the marrow. The terror is high-velocity, a relentless assault upon the flesh that confirms the precariousness of physical existence and the immutable inevitability of corporeal degradation.

Pillar B: The Small-Town / Cosmic Epic (The Banal Apocalypse)

This pillar inherits the demand for generational, systemic, and accessible evil, a construct forged by Stephen King, H.P. Lovecraft, and Shirley Jackson. King perfected the art of domesticating the monstrous, rendering ancient evils familiar within suburbia. Lovecraft revealed the cosmos's crushing indifference, positioning humanity as an insignificant mote. Jackson exposed the insidious rot within the communal, demonstrating how terror could fester beneath a veneer of normalcy. This lineage forms the unholy trinity for the slow, creeping dread that permeates the modern psyche.

The structural mandate for Pillar B operates on the principle of the Banal Apocalypse, grounding Cosmic Indifference squarely within the architecture of daily life—the grocery store, the mortgage, the cul-de-sac. The horror resides in the revelation that the mundane is a thin façade concealing unthinkable ancient evils or pervasive societal corruption. This pillar is reinforced by Octavia Butler's concept of Systemic Entrapment, which scales historical trauma into a precise Hierarchy of Logic, proving the "Monster" operates on dehumanizing rules that are entirely rational within its own destructive framework. The randomness of cosmic horror is revealed as the calculating calculus of systemic control.

Pillar C: The Experimental / Psychological (The Internal Abyss)

This pillar inherits the requirement for structural complexity and the exploration of internal terror, a tradition pioneered by Edgar Allan Poe, Arthur Machen, and Ira Levin. Poe mapped the landscape of internal mental dissolution with the precision of a cartographer of the soul. Machen introduced the creeping dissolution of sanity through arcane forces, demonstrating how reality could be eroded from within. Levin dissected the domestic sphere's capacity for conspiratorial psychological torment, revealing the insidious nature of intimate betrayal.

The structural mandate for Pillar C focuses intensely on the Psychological Perimeter and the Domestic Conspiracy, treating the human mind not as a sanctuary but as a Claustrophobic Architecture—a self-contained prison. Here, the monstrous entity arises from the fractured self or the systemic betrayal of the community. This pillar validates Octavia Butler's finding that the architectures of horror are built within the labyrinth of the mind itself, where reality is a malleable blueprint dictated by inherited biological imperatives. The internal abyss is a prison whose walls are reinforced by genetic predispositions and the relentless self-perpetuation of trauma, ensuring no true escape.

The Evolutionary Handoff: From the Cosmic Apex to the Algorithmic Void

The conclusion of Part IV marks the total saturation of the **Hegemonic Apex** through the architectures of Butler, King, and Koontz. The Unbroken Chain successfully maps every physical territory of fear: the cosmic vacuum, the suburban lawn, and the optimized technological laboratory. This era reached its structural completion with Octavia Butler, who proved that the ultimate "Cursed Space" was the biological self, where historical trauma and systemic entrapment are written into the very genetic code of the individual.

The handoff to the final era occurs as the **Physical Conquest** reaches its terminal point. With no more geography, biology, or psychology left to colonize, the Hegemony was forced to migrate into the intangible. The "Monster" is no longer a creature of flesh or a god of the stars; it is an **Informational Malignancy**—an unyielding data stream governed by an invisible, indifferent algorithm.

In the final chapters, you will witness the **Democratic Expansion of Dread**. The site of terror moves from the tangible body to the virtual interface, where the decentralized rise of the Independent Voice has bypassed the traditional gatekeepers of horror. The Unbroken Chain now enters the meta-narrative, auditing the collapse of truth and the omnipresent siege of the digital age, inaugurating the age of **Contemporary Virtuality**.

PART V: THE CONTEMPORARY VIRTUALITY

The Final Frontiers (mid 1980's – Present)

Chapter 32: The Domestic Rupture & The Ancestral Debt (1982–1995): The Intimate Siege of Sovereignty

The period succeeding the Modern Apex manifests as the absolute Internalization of the Void. A profound shift occurred; the vast, indifferent cosmos, previously an external terror, now compressed its chilling immensity into the most familiar dimensions of human existence. If preceding architects delineated a universe governed by an immense cosmic indifference, the architects of this era established that Intimacy functions as a potent, indelible Vector for Terror. The core "Architectural Handoff" relocated the Hegemony from the abstract or the distant into the deeply personal Proprietary Space—the home, the neighborhood, and the immutable bonds of lineage. This epoch systematically dismantled the final "Fantasy of Order": the false belief that any private space inherently guarantees safety. The sanctity of the domestic sphere dissolved, its protective qualities revealed as mere artifice masking profound vulnerability.

Thematic Anchor: The Intimate Antagonist

The structural innovation of this period manifests as the radical Transformation of the Protector. The traditional iconography of the monstrous underwent a systematic disinvestiture. In the sub-genres of the Domestic Rupture and the Black Southern Gothic (BSG), the archetypal "Monster" is replaced by a figure of inherent authority or irrefutable proximity: The Neighbor, The Parent, or The Ancestor. The horror is profoundly "Locational and Biological." One finds no escape from the encroaching threat because its roots are embedded deeply within the deed of sale, binding one to a compromised physical space, or interwoven with the very strands of one's DNA.

The domicile itself becomes a trap, and one's own body a conduit for inherited suffering. The key architect role during this era is the deliberate crafting of The Intimate Antagonist, for the source of dread originates directly from the individual who possesses the fundamental "Right" to occupy one's personal space. This era irrevocably proved that the true void mirrors itself in the human soul, making the closest relationships its most fertile ground.

Thematic Anchor: The Audit of Communal Apathy

Jack Ketchum (*The Girl Next Door*, 1989) provided the ultimate, devastating Audit of Communal Apathy. His architecture meticulously removed all vestiges of the supernatural, proving that "The Neighbor" can function as a high priest within a ritualized, systemic void. The structural evidence resides in the methodical degradation enacted within a typical suburban dwelling, its ordinary rooms repurposed for unfathomable cruelty. This stands as a definitive Pillar B (Moral Rot) contribution, revealing a structural flaw in the very concept of community.

V.C. Andrews (*Flowers in the Attic*, 1979) pioneered the Gothic of the Nursery. Her structural contribution was the precise localization of "Inherited Debt" to the intimate parent-child relationship. Andrews provided proof that the most effective "Cursed Space" is an attic—a sequestered domestic chamber—where the Parent operates as an Indifferent, Punitive God. The home's architecture, with its hidden rooms and locked doors, becomes complicit in the suffering. The synthesis of dread confirms the absolute surrender of childhood innocence to the depraved will of biological progenitors, exemplifying Pillar B (Moral Rot).

Thematic Anchor: The Precarious Existence and Ancestral Jurisprudence

Tananarive Due (*The Between*, 1995) brought a vital layer to the Hegemony: The Precarious Existence. The philosophical premise posits that current happiness can trigger an ancient, relentless debt, making peace a stolen anomaly subject to violent reclamation, and due to the localized "Cosmic Breach" within the Black middle-class experience, showcasing that the "Systemic Will" of fate acts as a brutal corrective force. The synthesis of dread lies in the conviction that one's present joy is merely a reprieve, a definitive Pillar A (External) horror.

Gloria Naylor (*Mama Day*, 1988) refined the Supernatural Juridical System within the BSG tradition. On the sovereign island of Willow Springs, Naylor engineered a "Cursed Space" that functions on its own immutable ritual laws. The horror is the Conflict of Sovereignty—the realization that modern logic is powerless against an "Ancestral Debt" that operates with its own unforgiving calculus. This narrative embodies Pillar A (External) horror, as a potent, ancient system of justice acts upon characters regardless of their modern beliefs or personal will.

Thematic Anchor: The Lovecraft Metric

Proprietary Nihilism defines this era. The grand "Vault" of cosmic horror is replaced by the familiar "Lawn," the claustrophobic "Attic," and the inescapable "Old Homeplace." The terror is rooted in an Entrapment by Ownership. Conceptual

Chaos reigns supreme; the rules of the family—trust, protection, love—are revealed to be "Self-Delusions." The perceived "Protector" operates on a logic that is rational to the systemic horror it embodies but annihilating to the individual.

The Body as a Battlefield becomes the final truth. The physical form is no longer an envelope for consciousness; it is a vulnerable Vessel for History itself, a living ledger of inherited traumas. Whether manifesting as methodical physical abuse in sterile suburbs or relentless spiritual claims in the South, the individual's inherent "Sovereignty" is systematically surrendered to the voracious needs of the "Legacy."

The architecture of the intimate siege is complete. The Unbroken Chain has moved from the external void to the domestic interior, proving that no fortress is secure from those who hold the keys.

Chapter 33: Visceral Complexity – The Body as the Final Frontier (1995–2015): The Anatomical Annex of Inevitable Dissolution

The human organism, a presumed bastion of self-contained existence, stands as the ultimate architectural construct, the primary locus of being. This era marked a profound departure from prior epochs that consecrated the domestic sphere as the site of ultimate terror. The architects of this period systematically revealed the Betrayal of the Biological; they recognized that the most terrifying "Cursed Space" is the human frame itself. These practitioners utilized the Transgressor Role to dismantle the "Fantasy of Bodily Autonomy," proving with clinical precision that physical existence constitutes a temporary lease held by larger, indifferent systems—viral, technological, or evolutionary. This structural truth positions the self within Pillar C: The Experimental Psyche, as the mind's construction of reality and its own physical vessel are perpetually under siege by these external yet intrinsically manifesting horrors.

Thematic Anchor: The Cellular Breach

The defining innovation of this era is the Total Erasure of the Internal/External Boundary. The Hegemony shifted irrevocably from "Environmental Entrapment," in which the house served as the primary prison, to "Anatomical

Entrapment," in which the self became the inescapable dungeon. The Structural Fact dictates that this horror is Intrinsic and Irreversible; one cannot flee the threat because one embodies the threat. The very capacity of the body to change, to decay, or to be overwritten by a superior "Systemic Will" forms the indelible source of dread.

This architectural principle establishes a terror rooted in biological inevitability, where the cells of one's being become the agents of one's undoing. The body's internal landscape becomes a contested territory where indifferent biological imperatives strip away identity. The concept of individual sovereignty dissolves; the body stands as a transient host prone to catastrophic failure. The dread emerges from the realization that the monster resides in one's blood, bone, and genetic code.

Thematic Anchor: The Funhole and Ontological Decay

Kathe Koja (*The Cipher*, 1991) pioneered the Architectural Decay of the Self. Her construction of the "Funhole"—a spatial anomaly and ontological fissure—demands physical and psychological disintegration from all who encounter it. Her work establishes that the "Void" actively invites the individual to be "unmade" at a molecular level, a total ontological collapse that echoes the Lovecraft Metric. Koja's vision of the self as a mutable, porous structure, vulnerable to internal and external corrosion, directly builds upon the existential terrors of writers like William S. Burroughs, translating the soul's addiction into the corruption of the cellular.

This architecture operates within Pillar C, probing the extreme limits of human identity. The "Funhole" manifests not as an external threat, but as an inescapable process of internal unraveling. It stands as a structural handoff from the psychological addiction explored by Burroughs, adding the specific wing of direct, inescapable cellular and ontological dissolution. The ultimate dread emerges from the fact that this disintegration is not only inflicted but also subtly embraced—a perverse communion with the void.

Thematic Anchor: Unreliable Biology and the Cognitive Breach

Caitlín R. Kiernan's The Drowning Girl (2012) represents the definitive Audit of the Fractured Mind-Body. Kiernan's contribution to the Hegemony is the principle of "Unreliable Biology." She treats mental illness and spectral haunting not as disparate phenomena but as a unified "Biological Taint," an intrinsic flaw within the neurological machinery. Here, the protagonist is incapable of distinguishing between a "Cognitive Breach"—an internal breakdown of mental faculties—and a "Supernatural Invasion"—an external force besieging the self.

This refined Systemic Entrapment, first explored by Octavia Butler, makes the "Hostile System" the brain itself. Kiernan appended a new, disorienting wing to this architecture of entrapment, where the mind constructs its own inescapable prison from its inherent vulnerabilities—a manifestation of Pillar C's experimental psyche turned inward. The internal world, once a sanctuary for thought, becomes the ultimate labyrinth of self-deception. This produces a dread that paralyzes the individual, for the very means of perceiving reality becomes the mechanism of one's own inescapable torment.

Thematic Anchor: The Lovecraft Metric: Anatomical Nihilism

Victor LaValle (*The Ballad of Black Tom*, 2016) performs a Structural Rejuvenation of the Cosmic, anchoring "Cosmic Indifference" in the "Physical Vulnerability" of the marginalized body. LaValle proves that for the "Other," the body is a target for both indifferent gods and brutal earthly systems, creating a "Double Siege" (Pillar A and Pillar B). Mark Z. Danielewski (*House of Leaves*, 2000) executed an Architectural Audit of Perception, demonstrating that the "Cursed Space" is a "Cognitive Virus" that infects the reader's mind. The book's non-linear structure functions as a "Biological Covenant"; once the information is absorbed, the "Systemic Rot" moves from the page to the reader's own sense of reality.

The Lovecraft Metric of Anatomical Nihilism reached its zenith here. The "Skin," "Vein," and "Synapse" usurped the "Hallway" as the primary sites of horror. This architectural shift revealed that "Self-Will" was a "Biological Delusion." The Final Exposé of the Body became the era's default resolution; survival demanded Transformation—an absolute "Surrender of the Human Form." The dread derived from the certainty that the self's physical manifestation is merely a temporary host, subject to forces both ancient and indifferent, ultimately subsuming individuality into a new, terrifying biological order.

By 2015, the Hegemony had successfully colonized every conceivable territory: the World, Society, the Home, and finally, the Body. This created an unprecedented "Structural Vacuum." With no more physical territory to conquer, the Hegemony migrated into the Meta-Narrative—the very fabric of story. This transition became the domain of the Independent Author, emerging from the KDP Renaissance to add the final, recursive wing to the house of cosmic dread. The physical world yielded its supremacy to the abstract space of narrative consumption. The Independent Author became the new architect, wielding storytelling as a weapon to infect the reader's reality itself.

Chapter 34: The Digital Threshold and the Rise of the Independent Voice (2015–Present): The Algorithmic Bastion and the Omnipresent Siege

The final movement of the Democratic Expansion dictates the transition from the corporeal 'Body' to the intangible 'Information,' a shift of profound and irreversible consequence. By 2015, the Hegemony had reached absolute saturation; its tendrils had constructed an unseen lattice of pervasive influence across every neural pathway. The traditional publishing gatekeepers—monolithic entities who for decades orchestrated the 'Architectural Handoff'—were comprehensively bypassed by a decentralized, digital revolution. This era represents the definitive Audit of the Algorithm, an examination of how ubiquitous, unseen processes govern the dissemination of dread. The 'Cursed Space' is no longer a physical location or a biological cell; it is the unceasing Data Stream, a torrent of unverified truths and fabricated realities. In this phase, the Independent Author has ascended to the role of primary architect, utilizing the lack of traditional oversight to explore niche, 'transformational' horrors that mainstream bodies deemed too cerebral or too transgressive for the collective psyche.

Thematic Anchor: The Decentralized Void

The innovation of this period is the full actualization of the Democratization of Dread. The Hegemony transmuted from a 'Monarchy' ruled by a select few best-selling masters to a 'Republic' of independent voices. This dispersal of authority intensified the horror, rendering it an inescapable murmur within the digital ether. The Structural Fact dictates that horror is now 'Omnipresent and Interactive'; it ceases to be a passive specter. The 'Siege' is conducted through ubiquitous screens, the fabrication of social constructs, and the immutable metadata that defines our existence.

Every digital footprint is a trail for the unseen pursuer. The Key Architect Role has devolved into the 'Anonymous Witness' or the 'Independent Chronicler,' figures who document the void from within. The source of dread is the 'Unverified Truth'—narratives existing outside official records, replicated through networks immune to scientific scrutiny. This truth is a virus, an infection of absolute certitude replicating beyond the reach of any antidote.

Thematic Anchor: Metaphysical Audits and Ancestral Malware

Current independent architects are pushing the boundaries of the Hegemony by positing existence itself as a malevolent mechanism of control. Their narratives systematically dismantle the perceived solidity of the cosmos, revealing a 'grotesque experiment' operating upon principles of 'quantum architecture.' In these structures, reality is a program under the indifferent, unseen gaze of a debugger. This situates modern horror within Pillar C: The Experimental Psyche, exposing the universe as a grand, flawed calculation. Individual consciousness is rendered a flicker of a moment within an unfolding, predetermined catastrophe—a mere data point in an inescapable simulation.

Simultaneously, the modern Indie Short Form is bridging the Black Southern Gothic tradition with the digital age's speed. These works perform an audit of 'Guilt-Driven Descent,' presenting ancestral debt as psychological malware—a parasitic code that overwrites the present and alters genetic predispositions. This places the Hegemony firmly within Pillar B: The Symmetrical Debt (Moral Rot), where inherited transgression is a bloodline contagion. The 'Short Story' format is used as a 'Viral Infection,' a narrative weapon calibrated for intensity and a singular impossibility to excise from the reader's mind.

Thematic Anchor: The Audit of the Residual

Contemporary independent voices are also conducting an Audit of the Residual, examining the lingering echoes of the Hegemony's previous manifestations. They explore the 'Static' left behind by previous architects, proving that true horror often inheres in the corrupted data fragments of forgotten atrocities. This exploration situates current work within Pillar A: The Invasive Breach, which addresses an external, persistent environmental contamination in which the informational atmosphere itself is tainted.

These narratives reflect the Lovecraft Metric of 'Conceptual Chaos,' in which the rules of reality flicker and are unstable. The dread is the gnawing realization that the present is irrevocably haunted by a past that refuses to dissipate—a constant hum of malevolence just beneath the threshold of conscious thought. The Interface, the Archive, and the Comment Section have replaced the Skin as the primary site of vulnerability—the new permeable membrane through which contamination flows.

Thematic Anchor: The Lovecraft Metric: Meta-Nihilism

The Lovecraft Metric has assumed a meta-nihilistic dimension; it transcends cosmic insignificance, declaring existence itself a pre-programmed terror. Conceptual Chaos manifests as the revelation that 'Truth' is an 'Algorithmic Illusion,' a curated hallucination generated by unseen processes. The protagonist discovers that their very act of 'Witness' is merely a segment of entertainment for transcendent beings. The only 'Fantasy of Order' is the clinical unveiling of the Hegemony's mechanisms. To endure the digital age is to

'Archive' the horror—to document the void even as it begins its inexorable consumption of the documentarian.

The Hegemony is no longer a secret history; it is a visible, undeniable structure. The 'Architects of Horror' have ceremoniously handed the tools of construction to the independent creator. The promise of independent platforms represents the fulfillment of the Hegemony's ultimate goal: The Total Saturation of Fear. Every 'Hidden Gem' is a new stone placed in the ever-expanding foundation of an inescapable, cerebral, and relentlessly permeating reality.

We stand now at the beginning of 2026. The 'Masters' have provided the tools, and the 'Architects' have drawn the blueprints, but it is the Independent Authors of today who are actively inhabiting and expanding the structure. The Ledger of Dread is a living document—a real-time audit of the 'Hidden Gems' carving new dimensions into the void. We now transition from the 'Why' of horror history to the 'What' of the modern exposé. We will apply our structural metrics to this new indie vanguard and dissect their contributions with academic rigor. We are now the Collectors, charting the expansion of an inescapable dread.

This cartography does not end with the final page of this volume; rather, it transforms into an active, ongoing surveillance of the genre's newest expansions. The "Veiled Archive" will continue this work through a series of yearly almanacs, serving as the definitive record for the modern era. Each new entry into the Hegemony will be subjected to the same forensic rigor established here, cataloged within the *Ledger of Dread* as a testament to the genre's relentless and evolving vitality.

These structural audits will be co-authored in real-time alongside the visual and auditory exposés produced for the YouTube channel, ensuring that the Unbroken Chain remains a visible and discussed phenomenon. By integrating these yearly records with the dynamic discourse of independent horror reviews, we move beyond static history into a living tradition of structural inquiry. We invite you to join us in this collective audit as we peer into the shadows of today to identify the architects of tomorrow.

www.ingramcontent.com/pod-product-compliance
Ingram Content Group UK Ltd.
Pitfield, Milton Keynes, MK11 3LW, UK
UKHW041635190726
13854UKWH00006B/2502

9 798995 224006